CLEMENTE

ELIZABETH AVEDON EDITIONS

VINTAGE CONTEMPORARY ARTISTS

VINTAGE BOOKS

A DIVISION OF RANDOM HOUSE NEW YORK

A Vintage Contemporary Artists Original, November 1987
FIRST EDITION

Copyright © 1987 by Elizabeth Avedon

Library of Congress Cataloging-in-Publication Data

Clemente, Francesco, 1952–
Francesco Clemente: an interview with Francesco
Clemente by Rainer Crone and Georgia Marsh.

(Vintage contemporary artists)
"Elizabeth Avedon editions."
"A Vintage original"—T.p. verso.
Bibliography: p. 79
1. Clemente, Francesco, 1952–   —Interviews.
2. Artists—Italy—Interviews.   3. Art, Italian.
4. Art, Modern—20th century—Italy.
I. Crone, Rainer, 1942–   .   II. Marsh, Georgia.
III. Title.   IV. Series.
N6923.C54A35   1987   759.5   86-40465
ISBN 0-394-74787-9 (pbk.)

COVER PHOTOGRAPH © 1987 BY RICHARD AVEDON

BACK COVER: *She and She,* 1982.
Pastel/paper; 24″ x 18″. Collection
Marx, Berlin. Photo: Littkenann.

Manufactured in the United States of America
10   9   8   7   6   5   4   3   2   1

AN INTERVIEW
WITH
FRANCESCO CLEMENTE
BY RAINER CRONE
AND GEORGIA MARSH

INTRODUCTION

Image—not an allegory, not a symbol of something alien: a symbol of the thing itself.

—Novalis: Aphorismen (1798)

Clemente invents what he calls "unknown ideograms, ideograms in costumes," in which "logic and chance as one force" become effective. It is to that intense experience, hidden in silence, devoid of words, where feeling and thought can be reconciled, that his pictures lead us.

Clemente's questions probe truth, reality and being. They are a response to findings in modern science, findings that have been investigated earlier in this century by philosophers such as Heidegger and Wittgenstein, and that, even earlier still, have been posed by the members of the Romantic movement at the turn of the nineteenth century:

> If the spectator could enter into these images in his imagination, approaching them on the fiery chariot of his contemplative thought; if he could enter into Noah's rainbow or into his bosom, or could make a friend and companion of one of the images of wonder, which always entreats him to leave mortal things (as he must know), then he would arise from his grave, then he would meet the Lord in the air and then he would be happy.—William Blake: *Description of a Vision of the Last Judgement*

3

Like the surrealists, to whose work Clemente's bears a superficial similarity, he makes images that startle the viewer. Unlike the surrealists, who directed their attention to creating a new visual vocabulary in order to elucidate traditional meanings, Clemente's images are pure inventions full of new meanings.

And whereas the concept underlying most surrealist art presupposed a certain knowledge of their pictorial sources, Clemente exploits figurative images for nonnarrative purposes. In this respect, he also departs from his more immediate contemporaries. Clemente's paintings do not tell a story, nor do they provide a description of a situation. Clemente's imagery attempts to unsettle the observer's conventional assumption of what reality is supposed to be.

It is in this sense that Clemente has something original to contribute: *figure-words*, as Novalis would call it, pictorial discoveries from a preconscious, prelinguistic world, releasing associations in the observer through the power of their expressiveness. This pictorial means is one we are most familiar with through fairy tales, myths and dreams—meanings of possible, conceivable worlds. His pictures question a reality that only exists by approximation, and whose existence we intimate through the power of our own desires.

R. C.

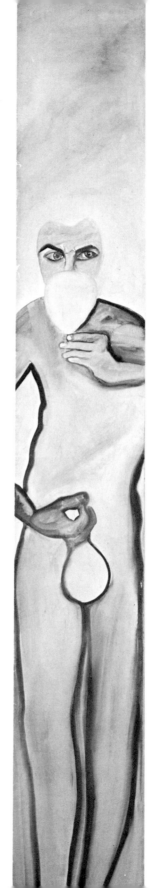

Untitled from "Inner Room,"
1983. Fresco; 95½″ x 13½″.
Collection of Charlotte and
Tom Newby, Neenah, Wisconsin.
Courtesy Sperone Westwater,
New York. Photo: Dorothy Zeidman.

THE INTERVIEW

RC: *You once said, "The world of our impressions consists, without a doubt, of memories. . . . This world's real center is represented by the self, by the 'I.' " And then you went on to remark that in the English language "I" and "eye," the physical eye, are phonetically identical, which you consider to be of major interest to you as a painter. I would like to begin by talking to you about your memories of your own life: about your childhood in Naples, your years in high school and your memories of your parents' home.*

FC: The first memories are images, aren't they? Like sitting under a table next to water on a bank. Or being afraid of a certain grotesque mask on a glass door in the apartment where we were living when I was two years old, and walking by so as not to look at this big face staring down.

Actually, I do have quite a precise feeling of what my life was like around that age. It was like a prehistorical period: enlightened, static. I see myself as surrounded by this gallery of shadows. I have an image of myself in the middle of this circle of figures. I don't know what the figures were about. I remember a sense of harmony. It was a very self-sufficient time in my life. Probably the most self-sufficient time.

I have no memory of the time after that. I mean, the more historic time, of school and so on. It seems like a plunging into blindness and forgetfulness; slowly the memories are less and less clear, and less and less integrating.

RC: *Do you remember something about the neighborhood in Naples where you grew up?*

FC: There is another set of memories, which is just what one is told what one is. I mean, I am told that I was the son of so and so, lived in such and such place, and so on. I belonged to an old family in Naples, grew up with paintings on the walls, sixteenth-century religious paintings, Luca Giordano, Solimena. These old families in Naples in those days, their feet were very light on the ground. I mean, they didn't really feel that they belonged anywhere. There is a view I remember, sort of an important view, again during the years before I went to school when I was six, of a garden, the garden of the Villa Pignatelli: it was beautiful. I remember trees swaying . . . things like that. These are the memories of an internal life. And I remember family types in the 1950s in Naples. My uncle, my grandmother. . . . I think of it now as a colonial life they were living, floating on the top of masses of people, flowing slowly across the surface.

RC: I would like to ask you about the publication of your book of poems, Castelli di Sabbia, which was published in 1964, when you were twelve years old.

FC: It was an embarrassing event, the publication of this poetry of mine. I had been reciting it to my mother since I was five or six, and it was published against my better judgment. It was enormously embarrassing, and it made me into a painter, actually, because I decided that to be a poet was too embarrassing; it was too revealing, and I wanted something more obscure to deal with. I thought of painting that way. That was about when I was eleven or twelve years old.

RC: What were the poems about?

FC: I think they were about nature. About seasons and weather and love.

RC: Was it more the eye or the I?

FC: No, it was more the eye. But dreams, too. Some of them are

8

very faithful records of that time that you connect with your dreams. So they are really about certain basic stuff that always remains. I can read them again and remember the feeling that goes on all your life through your dreams.

RC: *And your mother wrote them down as you recited them?*

FC: Yes.

RC: *Or did she . . .*

FC: I am sure there was no editing. I remember one—I don't remember the words, but I remember one—that is about, seems to be about a dream of flowers without hands.

RC: *I remember a recent painting of yours titled* Love, *with a couple, a moon and some clouds. It's very spare. That reminds me of some youthful dreams. I thought it was very poetical in that sense.*

FC: Well, maybe because that painting is about the weather. One has a sense of space. There is nothing there but the sky and clouds and moon. All those things are about the transition from dreams to weather and back to dreams. It's sunny, or it's rainy, or it's winter, or it's summer, and back into dreams. You know, dreams also have a very limited scope of mood. So it is a sort of transition. And my poems were all actually morning poems. I would put them together in the morning. And day mode, for a child, is dictated by the weather, basically.

RC: *So there was a gradual transition from the dreamlike stage during the night into the daylight stage?*

FC: It was like making a trip from one to the other.

RC: *So did dreams play a major role for you in your childhood?*

FC: Yes, because my childhood was very quiet, so the certain terrible side of life was all in the imagination, not in what was happening. What was happening was very plain, but I had a sense of predestination, and the only way to make it a bit more real was to look back into dreams, to substantiate it.

RC: I read someplace that when you grew up in Naples and attended grammar school, your preferred subjects were Latin, Greek, classical philosophy and Italian literature. Which one of these subjects really had an impact, an interest?

FC: I don't know. I mean, I don't know if my diffidence was born in those years, in the sense that in school whatever you learn and don't learn is not about what you are learning but is about something else. The teacher is using his knowledge to create a certain relationship with his students, and the students are using what they are learning to create another situation among themselves. So I don't know. But it might have been in those years that I learned to be diffident. I learned that if you sit at one end of the room and you are the teacher, no matter what you say, you are still the teacher. It is more about your voice and your position than about what you are actually saying. How much of that is only school, or is all knowledge like that? School is a prototype for secondhand knowledge. All school is about secondhand knowledge. And if there is an enemy to fight, it is the secondhand— whatever is mediation and not firsthand experience. So I really don't know if all that was born out of those years. I do remember being very matter-of-fact in dealing with all that. But at the same time I remember learning from other people. I found a friend who was homosexual and superintelligent. He wanted to be a poet but he had to be a lawyer. His family was famous for bringing bad luck, you know . . . they were famous for generations; so everyone would just run away from him. So he was really the prototype of someone who has to invent his own world. I remember hanging around with him a lot. He went to Lacan lectures way before Lacan was ever popular. I remember him talking about Lacan in those years, and writing down all the texts of Bob Dylan's songs, word for word. I have never been able to really do the digging work myself. I was getting a lot of ideas and information from him, and not doing all the homework myself.

RC: *You went to a humanistic grammar school that taught Greek and Latin. Don't you think it had an influence?*

FC: Well, perhaps, because I was sixteen in 1968, my generation was the last one that studied with these extremely old-fashioned teachers. I had a great Greek teacher who was the author of the Greek dictionary that was used in all the schools in Italy. They had this grand approach and behavior, and they were grand old people.

RC: *And a little bit removed from the real world outside, so to speak?*

FC: If I look back, they were a great generation in a sense. They were better than whatever happened after that, I suppose, because they were removed. So in a way it was an advantage, but it was also false. When one talked of Roman history one had to know about Cicero, and democracy, and about the Republic and how clean everything was. One didn't have to know about the decadence and the flexibility of thought; one had to know about the rigidity of thought. The whole point was that there are these rigid systems that work and make the world run; you had to know about that. You didn't have to know about things which make the edges blur.

   If you read history, you had to read a history of those who won, not of those who lost, so you read Tacitus and you didn't read Suetonius. You didn't imagine that history is a lie accumulated by the winners. Tacitus is about winners. Suetonius is the outsider, the lonely witness facing a hundred years of monstrosity and making some personal sense out of it.

RC: *You were born into a family of titled descent. Your father was a marquess and your uncle was Prince Clemente di San Luca. What*

UNTITLED (PAIR WITH DOTS), from *Il Viaggiatore napoletano*, 1977. Ink/paper; 5½″ x
16¼″. Collection of Oeffentliche Kunstsammlung, Basel. Courtesy Sperone
Westwater, New York. Photo: Courtesy Oeffentliche Kunstsammlung.

UNTITLED (SELF-DECAPITATING MAN), from *Il Viaggiatore napoletano*, 1977.
Ink/paper; 8⅝″ x 11¾″. Collection of Oeffentliche Kunstsammlung, Basel. Courtesy
Sperone Westwater, New York. Photo: Courtesy Oeffentliche Kunstsammlung.

was your parents' home like in this regard? Did you notice that at the time?

FC: Everybody is a prince in Naples. In those years everyone felt bad about themselves: the rich didn't want to be rich; the poor didn't want to be poor; the workers didn't want to be working class; the business people didn't want to be business people. That showed up with terrible consequences some years later. I saw it happening, and I was sort of just waiting, as I am now.

RC: What sort of consequences are you thinking of?

FC: Well, the seventies with the terrorism of an entire generation, more or less mine, or the one immediately after mine, let's say by a year or two. Actually, mine had a sort of more idealistic and naïve point of view during those years, and so maybe we suffered a bit less than the others. You know, up to 1970, Italy hadn't been so self-conscious, so European. There was still so much innocence, so much soul. But in the seventies, all that collapsed very tragically. Pasolini wrote a great article about this before he died. He discussed the sense of all these radical and liberal battles—abortion, divorce, gay rights, feminism—that went on in Italy, and showed that they were destroying this innocence. They were really the final blow to bring Italy into the European contest, which is a contest of self-consciousness, where the working class loses its identity and wants to be like everyone else.

RC: Looking back at these years in the mid- and late sixties, what do you remember specifically as the first political or social event of that time that touched you personally?

FC: Well, May 1968. That was it. Up to then I was painting, but for personal reasons, because that seemed a way for me to balance something I liked with all the things I didn't like. In 1968, all of a sudden, there was a great hope for change—all the things you didn't like might change into something else, and the artists seemed to be the people that were actually doing it, not the politicians. For one second, everything seemed to be in place.

RC: *At that time.*

FC: Yes, just for one second, and that second didn't bear any consequences. I mean after that second, everything was just the same; people just switched names and labeled themselves this and that. Just for one second. I never saw it happen again. You know, everyone could really say what he or she wanted, and you would believe it at that moment. Yes, I remember seeing things and believing them. I remember seeing a film with Pino Pascali lifting a Classical head from under water, or a picture of him right before he died, emerging out of a cone-shaped sculpture with someone holding a gun behind his head. So there was finally this sense of tragedy coming up, of having a reality, and having an answer of some kind.

RC: *Do you remember what happened at your school in Naples?*

FC: There were big fights, and people had their heads broken into pieces.

RC: *What about? About political issues?*

FC: Yes, about political issues. You know, wearing the wrong clothes could mean that you were beaten up the next day or something if you looked like this and that. Gangs of people, hired by fascists, sent kids to come up and break everything into pieces.

RC: *How about the 1968 film by Pasolini,* Teorema, *or Kubrick's* 2001?

FC: Yes, yes, of course. I mean, we all know what that was about, don't we? It was all very undifferentiated. For me the big discovery was that there were contemporary artists that I understood. I felt they were doing something and I wanted to be there with them. That sense of admiration gave me the push to take what I was doing more seriously in the sense that what I was doing was insufficient until the moment that I could use it to talk with these people on a valid level. I had a sense of the uniqueness of my own experience, that I couldn't really just do what they were doing, that I had to find my own way. I felt that it would take time, and it took time. But as far back as 1967 or 1968, I knew I liked things as far apart as Cy Twombly's paintings and Pascali's sculptures; but on the other hand, I just didn't have the tools to talk to them—I didn't know how to talk to them at that moment.

RC: So in 1970 you moved to Rome?

FC: Yes. And to the university to study architecture. At the time, everyone was trying again to find a place to sit. You know, we were in the middle of a conservative mode, no matter how radical the expressions in the work. People were looking for a job; they were looking for a place. They were looking for a way to exercise their desires. People were talking about terrorism, but it was not really happening. The original source of the terrorist movement was neo-Stalinist. The Red Brigades is a Third International sort of point of view, a pre-1968 point of view, but the practice of the Red Brigades is post-1968 in the sense that it is fed on the idea of total responsibility, that everyone is responsible for everything that might happen anywhere in the world. That was the soul of it, and then the water one swam in was a post-1968 skepticism. If you doubt the morality of the way things are produced, you end up being unable to believe anything. The social context of what you were making was wrong, and so you had better not make anything. A great talent like Godard ended up that way; he stopped making films.

RC: Cy Twombly's 1968 exhibition was, in this context, a major artistic event for you personally, and as an artist, wasn't it?

FC: Well, yes. Because of the political times, one felt that any work should have a political valence. I still believe that now; any work of art should have that political self-consciousness. On the other hand, looking at those Cy Twombly paintings, I knew that they had a tremendous integrity that wasn't in any of the Arte Povera works. One could say, of course, that Burri's work had the same integrity, but the difference, I think, is that Twombly had a more Mediterranean soul than Burri. You know, I am from Naples; I don't "feel" Umbria.

Somehow in Twombly's work you could breathe the Mediterranean spirit so much more than in Burri's work, which is really fairly local, you know—work from Assisi, from where St. Francis was born. [Every year in Assisi there is a public procession where they carry the rags of St. Francis out into the streets.] I mean, those were really the rags of St. Francis there on the canvas. There is more joy and more hope and more light, more Italian light, in Twombly's paintings than in Burri's. Having lived in America for some years now, I know now how political Twombly's work is—how extremely radical, tremendous. At that time, I had no idea about that.

RC: *You often refer to Aleghiero Boetti as a friend as well. An artist whom you highly respected and who introduced you to the arts. How close were you to him and how much influence did he exert on you in these early years?*

FC: Well, a great influence. You know I believe that art is really the last oral tradition alive in the West.

RC: *Oral?*

FC: Yes. Art is the last oral tradition alive in the West. It is the only sort of oral tradition that is not lost, and that's really one of the main reasons I am an artist, because I believe in that kind of learning and in that kind of tradition. Boetti is the person through whom I had firsthand information about a lot of the things we are talking about. His work was supremely eclectic, so it was through him that I was in touch firsthand with a lot of other work that I couldn't have used otherwise. I mean, if you look at Jasper Johns's work from the vantage point of Italy, 1972, what do you make of it if that work doesn't filter through someone else closer to your terms and to your situation? Or Joseph Beuys's work, or the minimalists? I could make sense out of all that through Aleghiero.

RC: *He was ten years older than you?*

FC: Yes. Exactly ten years older. I had endless discussions of ideas and of his work with him and his wife. The imagery, the iconography of his work was eclectic, covering ground from people as far apart as Jasper Johns and Bruce Nauman, and in terms of ideas, from the French philosophers, Lacan, Foucault, Deleuze, ideas of order, ideas of autonomy, and again, a critique of politics.

RC: *You met him in Rome, I guess?*

FC: Yes.

RC: *And then in 1973 you made your first trip to India, to Delhi, where you made your first pastels and drawings. Why did you go to India? Do you remember?*

FC: Well, India was in the landscape of the 1960s, wasn't it? But again, being permanently retarded and permanently late about all sorts of conventions and ideas, I didn't go then; I just went when it was all over. I wanted to be somewhere else, and I thought that was as far as I could go and I had the surprise of my life. I mean, I just couldn't believe my eyes.

RC: *What sort of surprises were there? That it was a non-Western culture?*

FC: Well, my opinions about it have changed so much through

the years that I am not sure I can really recollect what my first reactions were, but it was a radical change. Just the idea that people could eat that stuff. And, you know, the dealings with basic human functions, like eating and shitting and breathing, and so on. It was so radically different. The weight of those things was so different than they are in our life. Just getting off the plane, having the bellboy bring you to a room in a hotel, looking at you and saying, "Oh, you are not relaxed enough," and, on the spot, giving you a massage and making all your bones crack. It was such a surprise. That someone could pay attention to that and know what was happening, and have the time to do something about it. A tremendous surprise.

RC: You got introduced at that time to the culture, to the religion?

FC: I was carrying a translation of some conversations with me. I had a friend in Rome who gave me a translation of the conversations of a holy man who was living in Delhi. I sought him out and made friends with him and was his guest for two months. So I entered into an extremely lively and curious tradition that is particular to India, though analogous to the pre-Socratic tradition. It is an oral tradition concerned with correct behavior, with the fact that knowledge is a proportion between what you are and what you know. There is no point in having a knowledge that is not going to make you into a happier person, a happier . . . Let's see, how can I say this economically? There is a tradition concerned with correct behavior, which means that there is a proportion between what you say and what you are.

RC: Yes.

FC: The essential tools of this tradition are ideas that are close to the basic Buddhist message that there is suffering in life. The reason for suffering is ignorance. The beginning of ignorance is unknown. We don't know how ignorance began, but there are tools. There is an education that can bring ignorance to an end.

SYMBOLON, from *Il Viaggiatore
napoletano*, 1977. Ink/paper;
5⅞" x 7⅞". Collection of
Oeffentliche Kunstsammlung, Basel.
Courtesy Sperone Westwater,
New York. Photo: Courtesy
Oeffentliche Kunstsammlung.

symbolon

The reason for ignorance is desire. There is an education that can free you from desire. To be free from desire means to be free of the fear of death, and the condition of people who are educated in that way is a condition of freedom. This is basic.

This education is an accumulation of skills and techniques and teachings that are empirical, so they can be verified. The legitimacy of this teaching is given by the oral tradition, by a lineage. Each teacher is such because he has had a previous teacher who has had a previous teacher who has had a previous teacher, so they all have been in touch with this original feeling of integrity which they know about and can transmit.

Given this frame, there is an endless number of lineages of people who are concerned with this learning. The reason for this variety is that you must—since the learning is connected to an experience of love—you must be able to love your teacher. So to love somebody you have to like him. You must have all sorts of different personalities so that you can find the right one for you, and also all kinds of different sets of ideas so that you might be able to like the ideas. All this has nothing to do with a set of religions. It might, and it might not, have anything to do with religion. You might have a teacher who has completely secular ideas. It is really not about religion, and it is not about authority. In Catholicism, the authority of the pope derives from the fact that you just can't verify his ideas: you have to accept them. That's what is meant by authority. Whereas in this tradition the authority is such that you can verify it in the results that the teaching has on you. At the time, I was very surprised by the whole situation that was going on there between this man and his four students. I didn't really know what to think of it, but I was extremely impressed, watching these things.

RC: But his students were Indian?

FC: Two of them were sadhus, wandering beggars who give up all they have and grow their hair and beards and don't have any possessions and lead ascetic lives. Two of them were Western, a boy and a girl from Europe. So really there were two completely different groups.

RC: *So you were involved personally with him, with this group, for how long in 1973?*

FC: I was there, but I wasn't involved. I was listening to him and I was watching. I really didn't do anything; I really didn't know how to. On the one hand, these people present you with a fact, which is freedom and integrity, and that is a tremendous surprise. On the other hand, it is an illusion, and it is meant to be an illusion. When you question them, they tell you that everyone on earth brings this integrity with him, so you are put in a double bind because if you see what they say, you have to leave the next minute. On the other hand, if you leave the next minute, you may not be able to remember what they made you believe. The gift that these teachers have, in the first place, is that from the first minute, they are able to make you believe that this freedom does in fact exist. They embody this kind of freedom. On the other hand, they always point out the fact that everyone carries this freedom in himself, and you should be able to recognize it in everybody. The reason why they have students is because they offer some people a break, let's say, during which you give up the specificity of your experience and join a wider experience before you can get your specific experience back. At the time I was with him, I felt so strongly that I was an artist and a painter, and that that was going to be it for me, the tool to evaluate my social and mental habits, that I didn't think the time was right for me to be a student. On the one hand, I couldn't be with this person—in terms of being a student, that is. On the other hand, the fact that such a person existed, in a way, was the answer to all my questions about the political balance of a work of art. The work of art seemed a purgatory where one could give up what one was, while waiting to become something else. And this something else would have lost this mechanical character, and would have had the character of freedom.

The poet John Wieners was asked in an interview with Raymond Foye, "What are you doing now that you're not writing?" and Wieners said, "I am living out the logical conclusion of my books"—putting his poetry into practice. I think that is the greatest ambition.

RC: At the beginning of this question you mentioned the pre-Socratics. How do they connect to all this?

FC: Well, there is really an analogy with the oral traditions all over the world, with the pre-Socratic tradition and the oral traditions in India or Africa or in South America: they all seem to make this feminine spirit of Neolithic times survive—a spirit of openness, an empirical spirit in the true sense of the word. They make it survive; and that seems the true spirit of the planet. I don't think of the planet as masculine.

RC: When you left India after three months, did you want to go back to your work?

FC: Well, when I got back, the difference was so much stronger then than now. To come back and look at the dullness . . . the eyes were so lifeless, you know. I just couldn't believe it when I came back.

RC: In 1974 you went with Aleghiero Boetti to Afghanistan.

FC: Yes. Afghanistan was different, you know. It is a Moslem country; it was really out of this time. It was one of the last places sleeping in some other time of dignity, in a very static time. We are talking of a one hundred percent contemporary place when we talk of India. One hundred percent civilized—in our terms, you know. Everything is just social duty. It is all about men. Whereas what is left of Afghanistan is this extraordinary, romantic image of a beautiful people, and beautiful, gentle smiles in suspension. I can't understand why these sort of people, who are having a decent life somewhere of their own, aren't just left alone and have to be destroyed. . . . How greedy the world is! That's all I know from having been there.

RC: *Then a year later you had your first several important exhibitions in Rome and Turin and Milan and Brescia. What do you remember of your feelings at that time? What do you remember of these exhibitions?*

FC: Well, you know, it was dramatic. First of all, it was clear that I couldn't get along with the academies, the academic seventies. I had every single Arte Povera brahmin against me immediately just for the fact that I wasn't some sort of second-generation Arte Povera artist. A few people who were bored and were looking for things they could use to do some art showed up and talked to me.

And then I left. I was away in 1977 for a whole year in India, but then when I came back, a new generation of artists had been exhibiting in Italy, creating a big reaction, and they felt that I had something to do with what they were doing, so they showed up and talked to me. So no matter how low-key I tried to be, it wasn't low-key enough for that type of situation.

RC: *The work, shown in 1975, was not really paintings but objects and drawings and wall drawings. What was the rationale behind them?*

FC: At that time, in 1975, the work was made in two layers: one part was the activity of drawing itself, an endless stream of images that seemed to generate one another, and the other layer was the editing of the work. I was photographing the drawings, framing, enlarging and assembling them. The editing had to be all about distance. The purpose of the editing was to insert my work into the context of the artists that I respected at the time. I have always had this feeling—I still have it—that I didn't want to react to the context; I wanted to fit into it. I don't think anything useful is born out of reactions. Which is again something I could verify on my trips to India, because theirs is a whole civilization built on the idea that you should always be able to bring in everything that happens, and never build in opposition to it but only bring it in. By 1977 I realized that no matter how much I had tried to fit in, I had to give it up and be on my own. In 1977 the degree of fragmentation and bankruptcy of all the ideas and all the people I knew was so high, so tragic for me, that I really didn't feel bound to anything anymore.

RC: In fact the works that you showed in 1975 were quite different. They were objects; they were wall drawings of a figurative kind, objects of a more nonfigurative sort, slide projections of drawings, and the very subtle photomontages you did at that time or even earlier. Looking back at that diversity of styles, how do you see that today?

FC: Style is the weight of what you are. I didn't want my work to be. I wanted it to become. I was concerned with a mobile, empirical attitude. I wanted to invent a territory without enemies. Italy is not a collection of dilapidated factories, it is a unique deposit of marvelous paintings and sculptures, but how to fit into that terrifying past? To believe you belong to it is a delusion. To ignore it is ingenuous.

GM: Many people in the sixties and seventies were trying to "go one step beyond." There were the minimalists who wanted to radicalize all the gestures made before them, and then there was the conceptualist's fantasy of the dematerialized art object. There was a radicalizing line, a linearity that your work doesn't deal with at all. Is that part of your relation to the classical? To opt for it out of sequence?

FC: The strategies, the ideas that you are taught, remain in the work; it doesn't come from within—art really comes from the world. Looking at politics in the seventies in Europe in linear terms, in consequential terms, meant to face a no-way-out situation. The recent history of Europe is the history of defeat. So you had to step aside and just find something else. I think that is true

COLOR PLATES

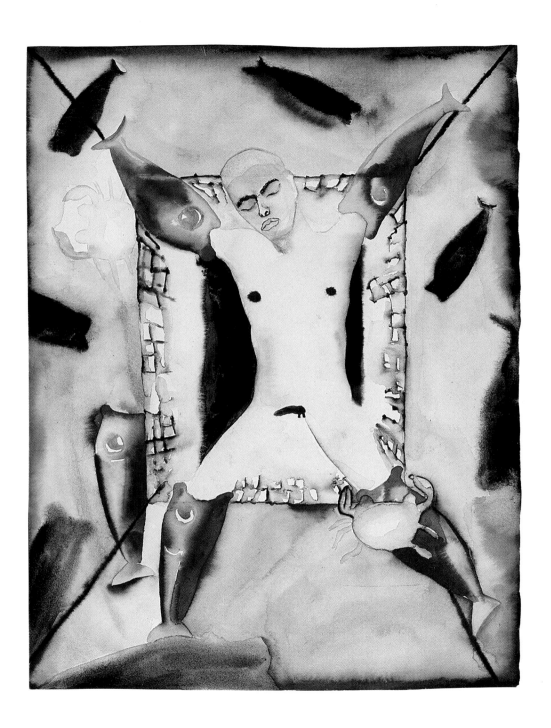

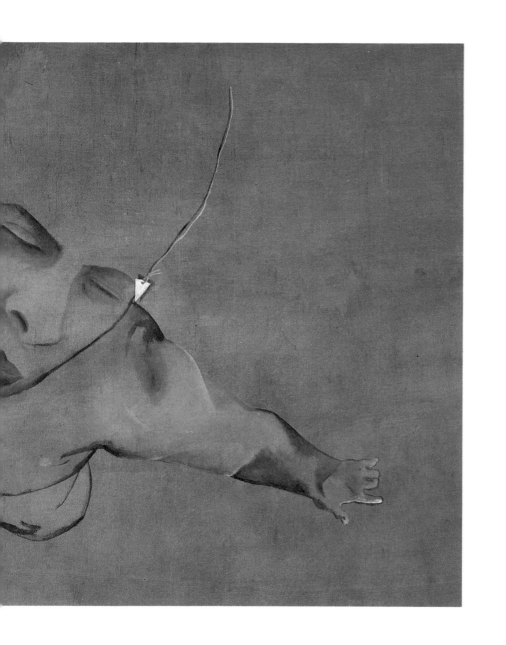

WHITE SHROUD, 1983.
Watercolor; 13¼″ x 17″.
Collection of Jean Pigozzi.
Courtesy Sperone Westwater, New York.
Photo: Christian Baur.

SEMEN, 1983.
Gouache/linen; 93″ x 156″.
Private collection, Venezuela.
Courtesy Sperone Westwater, New York.
Photo: Zindman/Fremont.

MOON, 1980.
Tempera/12 sheets of handmade paper
mounted on cloth; 96¾″ x 91″.
Collection of Alan Wanzenberg, New York.
Courtesy Sperone Westwater, New York.
Photo: Zindman/Fremont.

for the entire world. People believe they can recover an ethnic identity, that they are located somewhere and out of that they find a reason to fight. But it is really because they have no way of facing what is happening.

GM: *Like when you were talking about the history of those who lost— that history is a lie accumulated by the winners?*

FC: Exactly.

GM: *So are you opening up the space the losers lost. . . .*

FC: Sometimes to think of an experience in linear terms can really put you in a bind. You just can't go on that way, so you agree to look back in a very different way.

GM: *Do you mean that the biological metaphor in its linearity—birth, maturity, aging, death—doesn't really fit the description of what is truly going on?*

FC: That is an interesting question because that is not the only metaphor before our eyes. Another one is that you can look up at the sky and look at the moon and it goes away and comes back, you know what I mean? The sun comes back the next day as bright as before.

GM: *So this idea of ethnicity gives people a way, a very old and false way, of having a power source?*

FC: Exactly, a false way out, a false idea. But it says how little way out is left: all the lines have been broken.

GM: *Maybe it expresses the complexity of the choice more than the limits of what the choices are. Maybe the choice is so big, no one wants it.*

FC: Yes. You read the newspapers and you read what the politicians are doing and all that, and meanwhile the whole world is filled with ethnic wars. I don't know what that means, but I am surprised no one tries to find out. My traveling has been connected to the idea that in each place where I was, the continuity of memories, the tradition of the place, has been broken, somewhere, sometime; I don't know why. Really, you can't look at anyplace in the world from the place itself. You have to look from somewhere else to see what is there. In the seventies I thought it was Italy because of what was happening socially and politically. Then I went to India and I found that same degree, even more, of separation from the tradition of the place. And then I came to America and found another place that really can't come to terms with itself. One is afraid to go somewhere else to see it again.

GM: *So you've continually created that experience of dislocation and desire even though you talk about integrity and unity. Do you need that space of what is missing in order to make something, to find room for it? Or are you filling that space of what is missing? Creating a whole/hole?*

FC: Integrity and unity. Unity is something that happens: it's not something you can get; it is something that is given. There is no getting nearer to it; either you are there or not there. Distance is always the same.

GM: *Is that why your body appears in fragments in the work?*

FC: You keep going from one fragment to the next, and they keep appearing again and again, all these different forms of being this and being that. Maybe by accentuating this fragmentation you might end up opening a gap between all those fragments and just look through. . . .

GM: *The opposite of that would be succession and hierarchy.*

FC: The opposite of that is the pious view of the world, the one who goes out and seeks, deciding that those are the good things and those are the bad and then trying to suppress the bad things, and just put all the good things in a nice orderly fashion.

Just this year at the Kimball Museum in Texas, I saw an exhibition of sculptures from Donatello's time. I looked at it, and then I talked to the curator, and he asked me what I liked best in the show, and I said, "Well, I hate to admit it . . ." and he said, "Don't, don't tell me you like the della Robbia best of all." And I did. I loved it. I died in front of della Robbia. I looked at della Robbia and I felt like someone from central Africa who looks at those things made of dung and mud, and would never believe people thought this stuff was beautiful. I had to be that far away from Italy to accept the beauty.

GM: *What beauty?*

FC: I see the stains of blood on the blue sky because I know the history of those years, I know what happened, I know what has been happening. I can't just look at paintings as a sort of holiday, a vacation or something. You know, it is like reading Dante without knowing that he didn't have a place to sleep. I'm not saying this in a romantic sense, in a sentimental sense.

GM: *Beauty doesn't have to be sentimental and it certainly doesn't have to be lightweight. There is also an august kind of beauty, a terrible beauty, which you see in the blood in the clouds of a della Robbia. . . .*

FC: That brings us back to India. The Hindu tradition is specifically about witnessing events that are really beyond tragedy, beyond personal tragedy, beyond fear, beyond all of that. In the sense that you are saying that they are so terrible, you can't come to terms with them as an individual. Like Shiva dancing . . . all those terrible steps. . . .

GM: *Does painting have a place in there?*

FC: Yes. When you see Nataraja in the circle of fire, he is not doing anything terrible; he is dancing. It is an image made of calm, of beauty, of harmony, but you know that what he is doing is unmaking the world. Each step is a cosmos washed away. You don't have to *make* it terrible; it *is* terrible. It is a fact.

GM: *Can contemporary painting deal with that?*

FC: Ah! In the fifteenth century they thought they didn't have hearts strong enough, as strong as the people in Roman times. We are five hundred years older now. . . .

RC: *Let's go back to your personal biography, in 1977, when your first daughter, Chiara, was born in Piacenza. Did the birth of your child affect you?*

FC: Well, birth is really the opposite of death, isn't it? In the sense that all of a sudden you realize that not only can you not avoid dying, but also you cannot avoid being born. That was the discovery. All of a sudden I had this afternoon when this thing was going on, and there was no way out of it: she was going to be born, you know; and I just never thought of life that way.

RC: *And did this experience change with the birth of your second child, Nina, in 1981?*

FC: When you look at a child, you see where a lot of the images we were talking about are rooted, in this very economical message of liberation which is in the oral traditions of the earth, of the planet. This tradition, these traditional images, are rooted in the experience of birth and childhood. When you hear a child cry, you really know that people never stop crying all their lives. You really know that you are born with an impossible question; you have the feeling that that is all it is about. And you also believe that there is an integrity in people. When you see the first day of a child, you know that you are seeing the time of greatest intelligence of a person; there is only going down from then on, really.

RC: *In terms of intelligence?*

FC: In terms of intelligence, yes, if you talk of intelligence as an experience of integrity and of unity.

GM: *You've spoken of art as a tool to evaluate social and mental habits. You've also spoken about the integrity of a certain kind of intelligence and the morality of the artist. What is that?*

FC: We are schooled but have no teachers. A teacher is someone you learn from through a relation of love. I'm interested in this notion of right knowledge. In the Hindu tradition there is a word for knowledge, *vidyā*. The opposite word is *avidyā*, which is not ignorance but knowledge other than right knowledge, all other kinds of knowledge. Which means that there is a knowledge you can use to act correctly and which has a proportion and a relation with your being, daily, the way you are every day. There is another knowledge that has nothing to do with it. You can deal with it, but it is not going to make you act correctly. I have the impression that to write poetry or make paintings makes you face this question of what you need and what you don't need. We have to draw a line.

GM: *Art is a tool or a scale or a register of those different kinds of knowledge?*

FC: Before you make a painting you have to invent an audience, an audience for that painting. It can be . . . maybe it is you, maybe it is the person you love, maybe it is the community you imagine exists somewhere out there. So in that sense you have to draw a line between what you need and what the community you imagine exists somewhere needs. Later, when a real audience recognizes itself, you are sick of it and want to go on and imagine something else.

RC: *Let's talk a little bit about New York City and what your experience has been. In 1982 you moved to New York City, got yourself a studio, and shortly after that moved here permanently—with the exception of your trips to India and Italy, of course. How do you feel about living in New York?*

FC: Well, you know I discovered America when I came here. Seen from Europe, people think of America as a sort of intensified Europe, where all the things you don't like about Europe are at their utmost intensity. It seems that in Europe, people can't come to terms with the idea that America has nothing to do with Europe. It is really a completely different civilization; and having spent time in India, I realize that America is farther away from Europe than India is, and it is farther away from Europe than Russia is, you know. I mean, when you are in Moscow you look around and it looks just as if the European bourgeoisie finally got what it wanted. You come to America and the European bourgeoisie goes crazy; it thinks this is hell. For me, it was an enormous surprise. And the greatest surprise is the sense of good and evil in this country. Here, good and evil still have a meaning, and you just can't figure out why. Then, the answer came to me this year when I went to New Mexico and walked around in the desert and saw this very slight makeup the American Indians left on the desert, just this thin layer of graffiti and broken pots and a village. Where a village had been you see a slight curve; they just lightly curved the piazza around which they lived. Just slightly. Wherever else you go, in India or in Europe, you have foundations that go miles down into the earth. But here it seems that civilization has always, for thousands and thousands of years, been a matter of a very light film. Everywhere else there are a lot of layers, so good and evil get mixed with each other so many times it just doesn't make any difference now, whereas in New York this layer is still so thin. I don't think it's thin because it's new. I think it is thin because it has always been thin. It is just the character of what is going on here. It's heartbreaking, isn't it?

There is a tremendous pathos and spirituality of America that is just not understood if you don't live here. And also if you live here.

GM: *Pathos?*

FC: Well, that's really the distinction between Europe and America. Europe is really melancholic. There is no pathos. There is melancholy in the sense that in Europe the tragedy has already happened, that they have already paid the price. So what is left is this distance.

American songs and American poets have this tremendous integrity, this crazy hope of liberation. The un-European character of America was a surprise, but at the same time, coming to New York, you know what was missing, and why you didn't feel good in Europe.

But there is more than just thinness. I always thought of Andy Warhol as holding this tremendous weight of a thousand years of secular mysticism on his shoulders. He is more secular and more mystical—what is more secular and mystical than the Jewish tradition in Europe? What is more secular and mystical than someone like him? And then you know why there is a big silence over Europe; why, when you go back, it is so silent. You know why there are no songs. No songs, and there were songs before.

Then, still, there is one more element that connects with what we said before, and that is this innocence toward technology and the faith in technology that you find here. Technology has a lightness. I'm speaking again of the American Indians and the spirit of lightness over the earth, of being able to live on the earth with a light foot. Somehow technology has that character. It puts your mind in a very empirical state where you have to deal from moment to moment with new things.

There is a force of freedom, I think, in technology. If you look at technology as a product of man, it is the most terrible thing in the world and the most destructive. But if you think of technology as a product of nature, it is another thing. Not all other civilizations thought that man was at the center of the world, so the fading of this idea may bring some good things.

RC: *What are your impressions of the art community here, in New York City? Do you have any specific ideas about or responses to the art community, to the collectors and the galleries here in New York City?*

FC: Well, in New York there is a public for art which is analogous to the public for movies and includes people who are not involved with the making of the work. They are just out there: that was an extraordinary surprise. In Europe you don't have that; the public is made up of the people who make the work. Here you have an enormous public that is autonomous, in a sense.

RC: *Which is actually always the sign of a strong culture, isn't it?*

FC: Well, it is part of the continuity that we were talking about earlier that is the strength of the country—what Morton Feldman, talking about Broadway musicals, called the "middle of the sandwich."

GM: *If in Europe the public for culture is primarily made up of the people who are involved in making that culture and there is really no public beyond that, why do you suppose that is so?*

FC: I think that's a fact, with a few exceptions. There are really maybe two cities in Europe where you have a community around a certain museum or place; otherwise it's just not like that, like the community you find in New York.

GM: *There's no crossing between popular culture and so-called high culture?*

FC: There is no popular culture in Europe; that is the tragedy.

GM: *Where did it go?*

FC: *Al forno è andata.* It's too much to say; I can't say things like that.

RC: *What do you think of the gallery system in New York? Is it vital, productive? How do you feel about it?*

FC: Am I supposed to have a feeling about it?

RC: *How do you feel about critics? How important are they for you? Do you take them seriously?*

FC: (Sigh) They are there.

RC: *One of your most fascinating works is a very large etching,* Not St. Girolamo, *from 1981. It is an etching with aquatint, drypoint, softground and chine collé. Would you mind commenting on this print? What, for example, the individual scenes are, and what the implied meaning is if one considers the title* Not St. Girolamo.

FC: Well, first of all, I could point out some attitudes toward image-making. I believe images should always suggest a relative value within the economy of the work: the heavier the image, the lighter the medium, or the heavier the medium, the lighter the image. Then, again, talking in terms of overall strategies, what one seeks is an all-poetical language, a language that can include everything. In the Fenollosa book about Chinese ideograms, Pound described Chinese ideograms as an all-poetical language where each element of the language cannot be reduced and each element of the language is a link in a chain of meaning, ever changing and ever shifting. You can never see one of these elements by itself, but only in a chain of meaning and not for what it is but what it reminds you of: what it is not.

So, in the case of the print *Not St. Girolamo*, you don't try to focus; you are wandering. The images are results not of a focus, of focusing on a good idea, but of wandering from one idea to another without giving more weight to one or the other. The title, then, is not at the beginning of the work and not at the end of the work, but is just one of the steps one goes through in the making of the work. Since the work is an image, you can't tell where it began, and you forget where you began. So what you see there, I don't know myself. I made a safe; I invented the safe, and I lost the key. And losing the key makes the work, gives the work this autonomy.

It cannot be reduced. It cannot be brought back to its original elements. That makes it objectively poetical.

RC: *Autonomous.*

FC: Yes. This autonomy . . . makes it into poetry. Which strangely enough lines it up more with phenomena of literature than of painting in our century, because painters in our century have been more concerned with the reduction of painting. Well, I'm not.

RC: *Why not?*

FC: They seem to have been more concerned with formalizing painting into a language that can be reduced to basic elements, to abstract elements, with the hope that those elements have an inner reality.

But back to *Not St. Girolamo.* The title is part of this wandering from meaning to meaning and then from image to image. So you can begin from anywhere, from any kind of image, or any kind of activity, and just go on from there. And the title is just one step in this itinerary. On the other hand, you have a uniqueness which has to do with your personal experience. For instance, I look here and I see a knot, which then keeps appearing after that in other works of mine, much later or earlier, or somewhere else. I see a flag, I see a stone, I see a lot of familiar elements. I see all the elements which I do not control and which make this into something I made. I am not overly interested in those elements. I let them appear and disappear. Some of them may be made very laboriously or some very quickly, weak parts and strong parts. That has to do with irony, I would say. And with integrity. I mean, it is really at the opposite pole from Jasper Johns. Johns's technique to keep the world out of his paintings is to fill every spot of it with his best, with the best part of himself and his talents. Another way to get the same results is to show everything you are, to show the good lines next to the weak lines.

RC: *So there are meanings which one may or may not attribute to the work.*

FC: The meanings are an incident which you cannot do without; they are the way the world wants to come to terms with the work. But the work doesn't want to come to terms with the world. And it is never going to come to terms with the world. So the meaning may be a lie, even. To say *Not St. Girolamo* is to point out that there is an opposite to that. That the moment you give up all these notions, that one or the opposite is just the same.

The title is a way to smile to the critic and say, Yes, you have all these nice notions and they are part of experience, but experience is there without the notions, though the notions are not there without the experience.

RC: *Beyond this print now, in thinking of all the different kinds of techniques you apply: pastels, frescoes, lithographs, monotypes, etc.*

FC: All these different media have their given weight within a tradition where things have one weight or another. So you are supposed to make a major statement about your ideas in your big paintings, and you are supposed to take your leisure in your small drawings, and so on and so forth. But the point of the work is not to make a statement about the world, how you want it to be and so on: the world exists on its own, apart from all this competition.

RC: *Yes. But talking about the specific image in your work, there is this one from, I think, 1977, or even earlier—this drawing here, Symbolon. In connection with* Not St. Girolamo, *how do you understand this drawing?*

FC: I am not supposed to understand that drawing, given what I have said before, right?

RC: *I know, I know. The key and the safe.*

FC: I can point to a mass of reflections that have nothing to do

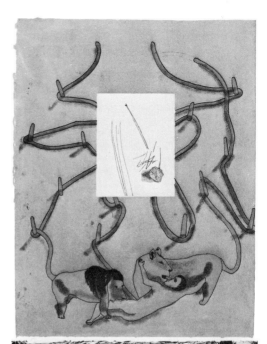

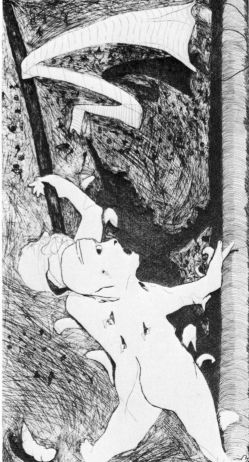

Not St. Girolamo, 1981.
Color etching; 63″ x 24½″
ed. 25. Photo: Courtesy
Crown Point Press.
Photo: Colin C. McRae.

with the drawing, and that is why I can point at them. At the things that are around it. The original meaning of *symbolon* was a coin that two friends would split when separating, possibly forever. When I made that drawing I was probably thinking of symbols as hostages of the Platonic world, and of myself as taking sides with whoever was at the opposite pole of Socrates.

RC: Let's come to another part of your work. In the late seventies you started a series, I think there were sixteen or so, of self-portraits in black ink. Some were very subtly colored. What is the significance of self-portraiture in your work?

FC: There must be a necessity to the work. Some of the self-portraits have to do with that, because if we talk about experience, then first of all we are talking about the commonplace. So what is the most immediate commonplace of all if not the body? It is something that everyone has, and no one can figure out what it is like. You think of the most immediate thing to you, and you try to think in the most banal terms you can, and what you come up with is your own body. You know, one edge of the room is the perimeter, is the walls, and the other edge is the skin, isn't it?

GM: What goes on between the inside and the outside of the body?

FC: What I say is that the skin is the commonplace between the space inside the body and the space outside the body. In a certain way, you imagine that it is the space in common. It is the space that the inside of the body and the outside of the body have in common.

GM: When you do self-portraits, are you saying that that is the space that the mind has in common with you?

FC: Here we are touching on one of the most dominant elements of the work: the interest in these two spaces, the space inside and the space outside, and the weights those two spaces have. You know, there is a landscape of the world and there is also an inner landscape of the world. It changes as much as the face of the earth has been changing throughout all these thousands of years. The landscape we see inside us in our imagination changes also; it is not the same.

GM: *So is the face a revelation of that landscape or a manifestation of it?*

FC: In these particular portraits I was really more worried about the body and the space around the body. They are called self-portraits without a mirror. It's really about the way you see your own body, without a mirror, in a sort of anamorphic way, distorted and fragmented.

GM: *What is the-body-without-a-mirror?*

FC: The body is what you see in the foreground. On the background you see infinity, the point at the end of the horizon somewhere. You also have to put punctuation in what you see, like commas; you look around and you look back at yourself.

GM: *So your body is a comma in the text of the infinite?*

FC: Yes, the body is a comma in the text.

GM: *That's the visual body. What about the other one, the one you know but don't see?*

FC: I like to see the body as the place between the external world and the inner world. That's where they meet; it's their space in common. And so we could say that the skin is the place in common between the space of the room and the space inside the body.

GM: *Is painting a skin?*

47

FC: Ah! A painting is a film. A kind of skin, yes. I don't know; if it was a skin, it would be a drum, no? I imagine it does have a sound. In Hindu tradition there is one word for space and sound, ākāśa. They describe all these different elements as oppositions. One of these oppositions is a point as opposed to ākāśa, which is sound and space at the same time. The point, the dot, is also like a seed. So it is the world before it is created. Apparently they alternate; it's like breathing for them. The universe is like this big breath going in and out. The making of painting has to do with breathing in a sense; the focus of ideas has to do with that. There is a feeling at certain times of your life or your activities which is really taking things in, and then you throw them out.

GM: *Can't those things go on simultaneously too?*

FC: There is a period of accumulation of ideas and a time of spending them.

RC: *So, having spoken about your work in the late seventies and about the different techniques, I wonder why you were so attracted by drawing, by works on paper rather than oil on canvas?*

FC: You have to find your own economy in your work, you have to do things in the most economical way you can. In personal terms, for the works made in India, the immediate reason might have been a matter of transportation of the works. I had to carry them home. The large paper works made in 1977 or 1978 involve an affinity with the materials—ink, paper, pastel. It seemed lighter, more discreet and open. The materials also implied a layering of feelings. Matisse spoke of that; you have to keep close to your feeling through the work.

RC: *In 1980 you first painted a series of oils, a series of self-portraits in different positions. Did you feel that the change from that medium, from the drawing technique to the oil medium, affected your work, and the meaning of the imagery?*

FC: I had to be far enough away from Italy, as I am in New York, to paint in oils.

RC: *I think that even these oils, and the ones that you did later in New York, touch the idea of immediacy.*

FC: Yes, they do. Even if they are very laboriously made. In a way all this history of materials is really a history of where I was. New York is also a Dutch city, and a capitalistic city. It is where the banks are, and banks and oil paint, you know, they go together; they have the same meaning and the same history. Oil paintings are the paintings of the banks; they are put away, you know. In the years when I was traveling to India, I simply couldn't have painted with oil. I couldn't have shipped the stuff back. It really has to do with my personal history, and the context.

RC: *In terms of immediacy and technique, again, maybe you can talk about when you came back to New York City in 1981, I think from a trip to India. You did a series of frescoes.*

FC: Twenty-four.

RC: *Twenty-four frescoes, yes. Rather large frescoes . . . portraits of your friends. Why don't you tell us about how they came to be, and how the idea came into being. I think that is quite significant. Tell us something about the technique of fresco, and the technique of watercolor, which is very close to fresco.*

FC: All techniques are the same in a sense. Really, the movement of the brush through all different techniques is exactly the same. What it is about, after all, is simplicity, how simple you can make it, how much you can simplify it. And again, the technique is also never yours. There is always a group of people around you. To paint a fresco in the fourteenth century, with fifteen starving twelve-year-old boys to make the colors for you and paint it as well, is different from painting it in 1980 in Italy, where no one is

Two Painters, 1980
Gouache/9 sheets of
handmade paper with cloth
backing; 94⅛" x 68".
Collection of Francesco
Pellizzi, New York.
Courtesy Sperone Westwater,
New York.
Photo: Bevan Davies.

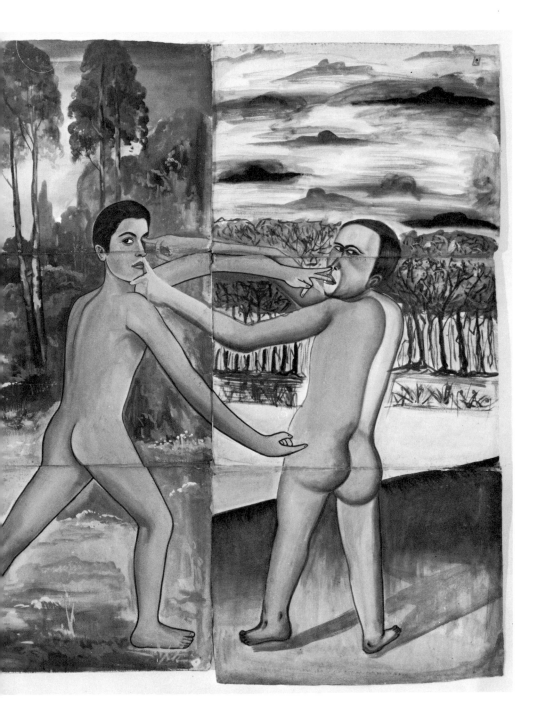

ever going to help you paint. In the frescoes you are speaking of, it was a case of, for me, extreme concentration and no preparatory sketches, no cartoons, and only having a feeling as a guideline. These particular frescoes are a circle of figures around me, just like those shadowy figures I imagined around me when I was five. There is a gallery of figures, each standing alone in some sort of exemplary attitude. I had a cast—I mean I had a cast director. Diego Cortez brought in people I didn't know at the time, actually. People would talk to each other and say, "Did you have your fresco taken?" like a photograph.

RC: *What were the circumstances in which it happened? You arrived here, and then . . . ?*

FC: Well, I had just brought works from India for a show, and I just wanted to do something here. Again, we are talking of circumstances, of making everything fit a need—which should be as real as possible. In this case it was being in a foreign city, and not knowing anyone, and getting to know the city. So this was a way of putting everything together. I had my show, and I met all these extraordinary people, but on the other hand it was a very formalized encounter. It was a very precise relationship, which I liked. It was something I could have left the next day, and I would have had a view of the city.

RC: *How long did it take you to paint these frescoes?*

FC: It depended on the circumstances, on who was coming, and on my first impression of the person.

RC: *Could you tell me about your preoccupation with book production, with books?*

FC: The books have to do with traveling, I think. They have to do with an image I have always had of Walter Benjamin getting to the border; he couldn't get across, so he killed himself. Whereas Max Ernst showed all these collages, and they let him go. It has to do with that. I always thought I wanted something I could carry in my pocket to get through the border. The point of carrying a book is that one book should be sufficient. Each one should carry everything in it.

RC: In that sense it might have a relationship to Duchamp's box.

FC: Books are a technique. The books I have made are about this feeling that the work should belong someplace rather than belonging to me. It should belong to a people, to a place, to an imaginary people and an imaginary place. To me, books, like frescoes, are born from a feeling of communality, exactly at the opposite pole from any sort of hierarchy and sense of what the use of it should be.

RC: So there is a close connection to graffiti, in a sense?

FC: Yes. You do it for a place, not for a person. And you think of the most economical means of survival for an art form, or for invention, or for a survival of the tradition.

RC: What about your recent book production? The most elaborate, I think, is The Departure of the Argonaut.

FC: Yes. Savinio has written beautifully about Italy as the last surviving place where the irresponsible soul of Europe is still alive. Italy is this place where things don't really need to happen because they are always there already. You know, what for a European is a conquest, for Italy is a gift. This is what Italians are busy trying to deny all the time, trying to make themselves into poisonous idiots, conquering things, which is not the nature of the country.

RC: Why does an artist illustrate written work? Is it a merging of words and the visual?

FC: It is not a matter of illustrating the written word: it is a matter of illustrating the heard word. Inasmuch as the ending of the text says, "Now the event should begin, the text must end." The text is whatever comes before, and when the real adventure begins, we have to give up the text.

RC: *So they are complementing each other rather than the one thing illustrating the other?*

FC: Well, there are all these taboo words in art: you are not supposed to illustrate. I don't know on what illustration depends. I don't understand what illustration is in the first place, so I don't know if I illustrated it or not. I don't know what it means. Don't you always illustrate your own thoughts in a way? Either you illustrate your own thoughts or you illustrate someone else's thoughts. As far as they are good thoughts, who cares? In a sense, one should always work on someone else's thoughts. There is always someone else who thinks better than you do.

RC: *One should define what illustrations are, if they are subservient to the given text, or if they give it a new dimension or respond to it in a totally different way. In that sense, if we look back at the history of book illustration, it would be interesting to know what you think of Matisse and Joyce, or Jasper Johns illustrating Beckett.*

FC: In the case of Matisse and Joyce, it seems a wonderful example of book decoration. In the case of Beckett and Jasper Johns, it seems a wonderful case of someone very clever who decided to put it together, but the two people by themselves shouldn't have had anything to do with each other. No matter how parallel, or precisely because of the parallelism between the two, they should be together in infinity, not in our world. They were busy all their lives keeping the world out of what they did.

RC: *When you look back at your work of the last ten years, can you characterize its main stages?*

FC: I guess if one looks back on the work, the main job is really to forget, and I really don't remember. The basic assumption of the work is that there is no progression; it's more a matter of being a witness to something that is always there, an attitude or a perception that is there. It is hard to describe what changes there have been, because it seems that stages have different things happening at the same time, and I don't know which line I should give priority to.

RC: A few thoughts about today's situation. . . . You've often stated that you have a special kind of admiration for Cy Twombly and also for Andy Warhol. They seem stylistically quite far removed from each other. In what sense were you attracted to them? Was it their work or their personalities?

FC: Warhol related with great competence to this very specific American situation of continuity between different layers of culture-making. He showed that his painting may or may not be better than a car. That was a radical political statement. But when we talk of Twombly, we talk again of how far you have to be from Italy and from that spirit to enjoy it, and to be able to make it talk.

We're talking about the political valence of the work, which, as I said before, is an absolutely necessary element for an artist.

Not every civilization had painting in the first place. Japanese clothes were more important than Japanese paintings.

RC: A few years ago you collaborated on paintings with Warhol and Jean-Michel Basquiat. Who suggested doing such a collaboration and what were the reasons for that?

FC: To work with an artist is a way to understand him. It seemed quite natural, since I had been collaborating with crafts people in India, doing the miniatures and books and so on, to collaborate with another artist.

RC: *You made reference to your Indian miniatures.*

FC: The miniatures were done by painters of miniatures.

RC: *And then you filled in some figures or what?*

FC: This is a discussion about techniques, and it really doesn't matter because techniques don't matter. They don't exist by themselves, away from the artist's view.

RC: *I want to talk about some painters of the past and especially those of your own culture—about Italian Renaissance painters. I remember that you mentioned that you admired Piero della Francesca. Could you elaborate on this a bit? What exactly do you admire in his work and why?*

FC: Paintings are simple things. They are important not so much for what is in them as for what is not there. When we talk of the Renaissance we talk of something very fragile; the surprise is that at a certain point, after a thousand years of Christianity, Renaissance artists looked at their bodies again, and looked at their faces, and looked at the world as a sensual place. This feeling of surprise happens again in Tiepolo's skies, and even down to de Chirico's earliest painting. If we talk of Piero della Francesca, what comes to mind is the light. There are two lineages of light in painting. One is a secular light: from Caravaggio to de Kooning. The light is outside; it comes down on things, and makes them what they are. But if we talk of Piero, or talk of Roman paintings, or of the Pompeian paintings, we talk of a light that comes from within and that has nothing to do with the history of man. It is a light that is before the history of man. Giotto is unique because you don't know exactly which way the light goes: his is already a completely secular point of view, but still the light is treated as an inner flow. There is really no one else like him; that degree of mystery is nowhere else. We have to talk in terms of light, because if we talk in terms of the formalities, what can we get out of it?

RC: *So what role, then, does Cubism play for you as a painter?* Les Demoiselles d'Avignon, Braque's *Grand Nude, paintings that stand at the core of so many concepts and styles in the twentieth century, are they important for you?*

FC: What is left of Cézanne's heritage nowadays is the necessity of not being at ease with what you are doing. The "modern" necessity of being what de Chirico would have called a bad painter. All the formalism that comes out of Cézanne, I really don't understand. I mean, even scientists have no hope to give us: why would a painter have to bother about that? It seems Cubism is still busy trying to give us a final picture.

GM: *Especially in twentieth-century painting, there has been a hierarchy of "who can make the last picture," who can make the most radical, the most absolute next step in the line. The conquest, the winners. . . . It seems as if you are stepping outside of this, not playing to that audience anymore.*

FC: I think that the main lesson modern art has given us is that Europe is not alone. To reduce the entire world to the European point of view is a betrayal of all the ideas of modern painters. The spirit of those years was fed by the discovery that people were making beautiful things all over the planet, with all sorts of different tools. What you have to be faithful to is the spirit, the feeling, and not some formal devices. Now modern art has become a formal device. You are supposed to glorify Western civilization against other civilizations, which seems like the ultimate perversion.

RC: *If one looks at your recent work, at your painting in particular, one finds the device of fragmentation—fragmented figures, parts of the body, and so on. Is this part of a larger scheme of intention, or does it just happen?*

FC: It is a strategy that has to do with what we were just talking about. Fragmentation has to do with shifting the attention from

TRADITIONAL SUBJECT, 1980. Oil/canvas; 22″ x 30″. Private collection. Courtesy Sperone Westwater, New York. Photo: Zindman/Fremont.

the way things look to the way things are made, and inventing a territory *in between* that doesn't belong to any known taste or device.

RC: Does this technique of fragmentation relate to the device of the dilettante? I heard you once admiring De Quincey and Savinio, being dilettantes, the latter being the brother of de Chirico, who was the "real" painter. Or does it have to do with memory, fragments as memories?

FC: Both. It has to do with the idea of the self, which is that you cannot trust any part of the self as the one that has to be in charge, so you have to give up techniques of integration, psychoanalytical techniques that favor one side or another. Art should really have this: every time, you should ask the question "Is it necessary? Do we need art at all?" And maybe your answer should be "no," and that is why the dilettante is there: because the dilettante is just doing it for himself. On another level, though, to ask if art is necessary is a false question, and the pretension to be a dilettante is a lie.

RC: And you think of that as fragmented?

FC: Well, the technique of fragmentation is on the other hand a political stand, since all parties are working toward destruction of the earth, the destruction of animal life, the destruction of the diversity of cultures, destruction of the diversity of sexes, destruction of all diversities. So someone who wants to be political in this direction has to be a dilettante. He can't belong to any group, because all groups are working in the same direction. On the other hand, in the private sense again, all techniques we have been taught, psychoanalytical techniques and so on, are all about making all these pieces into one thing that is under control, which you can hold tight to throughout your life. Maybe one can try the opposite, and just let it go to pieces. So the model of fragmentation might be a strategy for survival, for freedom.

RC: *Do you see the quality of a dilettante in Joseph Beuys's work?*

FC: No, Joseph Beuys seems the archetype of the grown-up artist. That's on the one hand; on the other hand, he is sort of the joker in the deck. He is the clown. So I wouldn't call him a dilettante; I would call him a joker.

RC: *Beuys remarked that physicists, at a certain time, practiced alchemy. He said, "Alchemy does not represent, after all, the beginning of chemistry, but stands at the end of a very long tradition of physics."*

FC: Maybe the elements that the physicist is dealing with are just as alive as we are. And, as far as consciousness is concerned, maybe an eagle might have more consciousness than we do, and the earth might have as much consciousness as we do. Physicists aren't necessarily dealing with dead matter.

RC: *What is your view of the rational force in life?*

FC: I think the rational mind is a form of imagination. The weak point of the rational mind is not to think of itself as a form of imagination. The artist's job is to bring back the consciousness that nothing is really necessary, and that rational things, rational decisions and facts and events, are not any more necessary than imaginary things. They are just more substantial. Not all societies have given such an importance to substantial things. Everything is real, and everything changes; this is the basic idea. There are some things that are more substantial than others, but all things are real to the same degree. An artist is dealing with imagination, and is dealing with things that are not as substantial as gunshots, but they are as real as gunshots, and they do have an effect much as gunshots have.

If people could think of works of art and atomic bombs and social structures as having the same degree of reality in them, we would make a tremendous step forward in terms of living. This is what Beuys was talking about when he was involved in politics and was elected to office. Why would he say "I am a sculptor" when he was going to an election? Not that sculpture is as real as an election, but elections are as real as sculpture.

RC: Do you see a relationship between mythology and the kind of thoughts you just expressed?

FC: It could be a step forward to realize that the rational picture of the world is also an imagination; it has the same reality as a myth. It is a product of the mind; it is not more substantial than the mind.

When we talk about mythology we are talking about questions of history, of rational thought and rationalized memory of our past. History is the most tragic product of the rational mind—a picture from which there is no way to escape. The picture of the world that history gives us is the picture of a dead person who looks over his own life. It is as if we are all dead, and we are looking at the world in a glass case. How can we get away from this? I have no answer for it.

May 13, 1986
Artist's studio, N.Y.C.

APPENDIX

FRANCESCO CLEMENTE PINXIT (DETAIL), 1581–1981. 24 miniatures, each natural pigment on paper; approximately 8¾″ x 6″. The Virginia Museum of Fine Arts, Sydney and Frances Lewis collection. Courtesy Sperone Westwater, New York. Photo: Alan Zindman.

SOLO EXHIBITIONS

1971   First exhibition in Rome.

1974   Galleria Area, Florence.

1975   Gian Enzo Sperone, Rome.
       Massimo Minimi, Brescia.
       Franco Toselli, Milan.

1976   Gian Enzo Sperone, Rome.
       Lucrezia de Dominizio, Pescara.

1977   Paola Betti, Milan.

1978   Centre d'Art Contemporain, Geneva.
       Art & Project, Amsterdam.
       Paul Maenz, Cologne.

1979   Art & Project, Amsterdam.
       Lisson Gallery, London.
       Emilio Mazzoli, Modena.
       Giuliana de Crescenzo, Rome.
       Lucio Amelio, Naples.
       Gian Enzo Sperone, Turin.
       Paul Maenz, Cologne.

1980   Sperone Westwater Fischer, New York.
       Paul Maenz, Cologne.
       Padiglione d'Arte Contemporanea di Milano, Milan.

Art & Project, Amsterdam.
Mario Diacono, Rome.
Gian Enzo Sperone, Rome.

1981   Sperone Westwater Fischer, New York.
Museum van Hedendaagse Kunst, Ghent.
Anthony d'Offay, London.
Bruno Bischofberger, Zürich.

1981/82   "Francesco Clemente/Matrix 46," University Art
Museum, Berkeley, traveled; "Centric I: Francesco
Clemente," The Art Museum and Galleries, California
State University, Long Beach; "Francesco Clemente/
Matrix 70," Wadsworth Athenaeum, Hartford.
1982   Daniel Templon, Paris.
"Il viaggiatore napoletano," Paul Maenz, Cologne.
Mario Diacono, Rome.

1982/83   Bruno Bischofberger, Zürich.

1983   "Francesco Clemente: The Fourteen Stations,"
Whitechapel Art Gallery, London; traveled to:
Groninger Museum, Groningen; Badischer
Kunstverein, Karlsruhe; Moderna Museet, Stockholm;
Galerie d'Art Contemporain des Musées de Nice, Nice.
Anthony d'Offay and Gian Enzo Sperone, London.
Mario Diacono, Rome.
"Francesco Clemente: Drawings," A Space, Toronto.
Sperone Westwater and Mary Boone Gallery, New York.
Akira Ikeda Gallery, Nagoya and Tokyo.
Kunsthalle Basel, Basel.
Ascan Crone Gallery, Hamburg.
James Corcoran Gallery, Los Angeles.
"Pastels 1973–1983," The Fruitmarket Gallery,
Edinburgh.
Arts Council Gallery, Belfast.

1984/85 "Francesco Clemente, Pastels," Nationalgalerie, Berlin;
     Museum Folkwang, Essen; Stedelijk Museum,
     Amsterdam; Kunsthalle Tübingen, Tübingen.
     Kestner-Gesellschaft, Hannover.
     Akira Ikeda Gallery, Tokyo.

  1985 Sperone Westwater and Leo Castelli, New York.
     Mary Boone Michael Werner, New York.
     Bruno Bischofberger, Zürich.
     "Francesco Clemente Prints 1981–1985," The Mezzanine
     Gallery, The Metropolitan Museum of Art, New York.

1985/87 "Francesco Clemente," The John and Mable Ringling
     Museum of Art, Sarasota; Walker Art Center,
     Minneapolis; Dallas Museum of Art, Dallas; University
     Art Museum, Berkeley; The Albright-Knox Art
     Gallery, Buffalo; Museum of Contemporary Art,
     Los Angeles.

  1986 14th Biennial, Adelaide Festival of Arts, Adelaide.
     "Woman and Men, Watercolors," Akira Ikeda Gallery,
     Tokyo.
     Anthony d'Offay, London.
     Sperone Westwater, New York.
     "Francesco Clemente: The Departure of the Argonaut,"
     The Museum of Modern Art, New York.

FRANCESCO CLEMENTE PINXIT (DETAIL), 1581–1981. 24 miniatures, each natural pigment on paper; approximately 8¾″ x 6″. The Virginia Museum of Fine Arts, Sydney and Frances Lewis collection. Courtesy Sperone Westwater, New York. Photo: Alan Zindman.

GROUP EXHIBITIONS

1973   "Italy Two," Civic Center Museum, Philadelphia.

1974   Studenteski Center, Belgrade.

1975   XII Biennale, São Paulo.
       "24 Hours out of 24," Galleria l'Attico, Rome.
       "Campo Dieci," Galleria Diagrama, Milan.

1976   "Merz, Pisani, Clemente," Gian Enzo Sperone, Rome.

1977   "Drawings/Transparency," Studio Cannaviello, Rome.
       "Wednesday 16 February 1977," Gian Enzo Sperone,
          Rome.
       Xe Biennale de Paris, Musée d'Art Moderne, Paris.
       "Progetto 80," Bari.

1978   "Pas de deux," Galleria la Salita, Rome.

1979   "Perspective 79," Basel Art Fair, Basel.
       "Arte Cifra," Paul Maenz, Art Fair, Cologne.
       "Clemente, de Maria, Paladino," Annemarie Verna,
          Zürich.
       "Europa 79," Stuttgart.
       "Parigi, O Cara . . . ," Yvon Lambert, Paris.
       "Opere Fatte ad Arte," Palazzo di Citta, Acireale.
       "Le Stanze," Colonna Castel, Genazzano.

1980   "The Cut-Off Hand—100 Drawings from Italy"
          (title translated), Bonner Kunstverein, Bonn; Stad-

tische Galerie, Wolfsburg; Groninger Museum,
   Groningen.
"Egonavigatio," Kunstverein, Mannheim.
Francesco Masnata, Genoa.
"Aperto '80," Venice Biennale, Venice.
Kunsthalle Basel, Basel; Museum Folkwang, Essen;
   Stedelijk Museum, Amsterdam.
Sperone Westwater Fischer, New York.
"Neuerwerbungen," Galerie Rudolph Zwirner, Cologne.

1981   Group Show, Daniel Templon, Paris.
   Gian Enzo Sperone, Turin.
   "Westkunst," Rheinhallen der Kölner Messe, Cologne.
   Paola Betti, Milan.
   "Italians and American Italians," Crown Point Gallery,
      Oakland, California.
   "L'Identité Italienne: Art en Italie depuis 1959," Musée
      d'Art Moderne, Centre Georges Pompidou, Paris.
   Sperone Westwater Fischer, New York.
   "Figures: Forms and Expressions," Buffalo (sponsored
      jointly by The Albright-Knox Art Gallery, CEPA
      Gallery, and Hallwalls).
   "Large Format Drawings," Barbara Toll Fine Arts, New
      York.
   "Tesoro," Emilio Mazzoli, Modena.
   "Aspects of Post-Modernism," The Squibb Gallery,
      Princeton, New Jersey.

1982   "Issues: New Allegory I," Institute of Contemporary Art,
      Boston.
   Documenta 7, Kassel.
   "Homo Sapiens: the many images," The Aldrich Museum
      of Contemporary Art, Ridgefield, Connecticut.
   "The Pressure to Paint," Marlborough Gallery, New York.
   "Five Painters: Chia, Clemente, Kiefer, Salle, Schnabel,"
      Anthony d'Offay, London.

"New Work on Paper 2: Borofsky, Clemente, Merz,
    Penck, Penone," The Museum of Modern Art, New
    York.
"kunst nu/kunst unserer zeit," Kunsthalle Wilhelmshave,
    and Groninger Museum, Groningen.
"Avanguardia Transavanguardia 68, 77," Mura Aureliane,
    Rome.
Emilio Mazzoli, Modena.
"Zeitgeist," Walter Gropius Bau, Berlin.
"How to Draw / What to Draw: Works on Paper by Five
    Contemporary Artists," The Parrish Art Museum,
    Southampton, New York.

1982/83   Rosa Esman Gallery, New York.
          "Myth," The Bonlow Gallery, New York.

    1983 "New Italian Art," The New Gallery of Contemporary
              Art, Cleveland.
          "Trustee's Choice," The Aldrich Museum of
              Contemporary Art, Ridgefield, Connecticut.
          "Chia, Clemente, Cucchi," Kunsthalle Bielefeld,
              Bielefeld, West Germany, and Louisiana Museum,
              Humlebaek, Denmark.
          "Artists from Sperone Westwater Fischer Inc.," SVC/Fine
              Arts Gallery, University of South Florida, Tampa.
          "New Image/Pattern & Decoration," Kalamazoo Institute
              of Arts, Kalamazoo.
          "Concetto-Imago: Generationswechsel in Italien," Bonner
              Kunstverein, Bonn.
          Bruno Bischofberger, Zürich.
          Nigel Greenwood, London.
          "Intoxication," Monique Knowlton, New York.
          "Italia: La Transavanguardia," Caja de Pensiones, Madrid.
          "Surreal," Robert Miller, New York.
          "Expressionist Painting Beyond Picasso," Basel Art Fair
              (Galerie Beyeler), Basel.

"The Painterly Figure," The Parrish Art Museum, Southampton, New York.
"Recent European Painting," The Solomon R. Guggenheim Museum, New York.
Emilio Mazzoli, Modena.
"Self Portraits," Linda Farris Gallery, Seattle; traveled to Los Angeles Municipal Art Gallery, Los Angeles.
Moderna Museet, Stockholm.
"Self Image," Sharpe Gallery, New York.
"Ars 83 Helsinki," Ateneumin Taidemuseo, Helsinki.
"New Art," The Tate Gallery, London.
"The First Show," The Museum of Contemporary Art, Los Angeles.
"Expressive Malerie nach Picasso," Galerie Beyeler, Basel.
Mary Boone Michael Werner, New York.
"Hemispheres," visual element in conjunction with Molissa Fenley performance at the Next Wave Festival, Brooklyn Academy of Music, Brooklyn.
"Sakowitz Festival del Designo Italiano," Sakowitz, Houston, Texas.
Anthony d'Offay, London.
"Det Italienska Avantgardet," The Boibrono Gallery, Stockholm.

1984   "The Folding Image," National Gallery of Art, Washington, D.C.
The Institute of Contemporary Art, Boston.
Galierie Leger, Malmö, Denmark.
"Made in NYC/LA," Galerie Amak, Berlin.
"Modern Expressionists," Sidney Janis Gallery, New York.
"Rosc '84," The Guinness Hop Store, Dublin.
"Totem," Bonnier Gallery, New York.
"Painting Now," Akira Ikeda Gallery, Nagoya.
"Det Italienska Transavantgardet," Stockholm Art Fair, Stockholm, and Lunds Konsthall, Lund, Sweden.
"Via New York," Musée d'Art Contemporain, Montréal.

Antiope—France, Paris.

Sperone Westwater, New York.

Anthony d'Offay, London.

Eaton Schoen Gallery, San Francisco.

"Drawings," Mary Boone Michael Werner, New York.

Blum Hellman, New York.

"Terrae Motus," Villa Campolieto, Naples.

"Portraits," Silvia Menzel, Berlin.

"Contemporary Italian Masters," Chicago Public Library Cultural Center in conjunction with the Renaissance Society of the University of Chicago, Chicago.

"The Human Condition, San Francisco Museum of Modern Art Biennial III," The San Francisco Museum of Art, San Francisco.

"Collaborations, Basquiat, Clemente, Warhol," Bruno Bischofberger, Zürich.

"An International Survey of Recent Painting and Sculpture," The Museum of Modern Art, New York.

"Painting Now," Kitakyushu Municipal Museum of Art, Kitakyushu, Japan.

"Content: A Contemporary Focus, 1974–1984," The Hirshhorn Museum and Sculpture Garden, Washington, D.C.

1984/85   "Images and Impressions," The Walker Art Center, Minneapolis; traveled to The Institute of Contemporary Art, Philadelphia.

1985   XXIIe Biennale de Paris, Grande Halle du Parc de la Villette, Paris.

"Drawings," Lawrence Oliver, Philadelphia.

"Graphics," Herbert Palmer, Los Angeles.

"Collaborations, Basquiat, Clemente, Warhol," Akira Ikeda Gallery, Tokyo.

"Selections from the William J. Hokin Collection," Museum of Contemporary Art, Chicago.

"7000 Eichen," Kunsthalle Tübingen, Tübingen.
"DIALOG," The Gulbenkian Foundation, Lisbon.
"States of War," Seattle Art Museum, Seattle.
Kunsthalle Basel, Basel.
"Unique Books," Anthony d'Offay, London.
"India and the Contemporary Artist," The Museum of
    Modern Art, New York.

CILINDRONE, 1984.
Collaboration: Jean-Michel Basquiat,
Francesco Clemente, Andy Warhol.
Oil crayon, silkscreen,
acrylic/canvas; 48″ x 66″.
Collection of Bruno Bischof-
berger, Kusnacht, Zürich.
Photo: Beth Phillips.

BIBLIOGRAPHY

Banco, ed. 6 *fotografie*. Brescia, 1974.

Oliva, Achille Bonito. *The Different Avantgarde Europe/America*. Deco, Milan, 1976.

Gratis. Genoa, 1978.

Undae Clemente Flamina Pulsae. Art & Project, Amsterdam, 1978.

Oliva, Achille Bonito. *Vetta*. Emilio Mazzoli, Modena, 1979.

Non Scopa. Gian Enzo Sperone, Turin, 1979.

Celant, Germano. "The Italian Experience—Touched Upon." In *Paul Maenz Jahresbericht, 1978*. Paul Maenz, Cologne, 1979.

Ammann, Jean-Christophe. "Expansive/Excessive." *Domus*, April 1979, p. 45.

Faust, Wolfgang Max. *Arte Cifra*. Paul Maenz, Cologne, 1979.

Oliva, Achille Bonito. "The Italian Trans-Avantgarde." Translated by Michael Moore. *Flash Art*, October/November 1979, pp. 17–20.

Faust, Wolfgang Max, "The Cut-Off Hand"; Oliva, Achille Bonito, "New Subjectivity"; Jochimsen, Margarethe, "Springboard into Metaphysics." In *The Cut-Off Hand—100 Drawings from Italy*. Bonner Kunstverein, Bonn; Stadtische Galerie, Wolfsburg; Groninger Museum, Groningen, 1980. (All titles translated.)

———. Essay in *Paul Maenz Jahresbericht, 1980*. Paul Maenz, Cologne, 1980, p. 10.

Ruth, Barnaby. Review. *Art/World*, April 19/May 17, 1980, pp. 10–11.

Maenz, Paul, ed. *Egonavigatio*, Cologne, 1980.

Oliva, Achille Bonito. "The Bewildered Image." *Flash Art*, March/April 1980, pp. 32–35, 38–39, 41.

Rickey, Carrie. "Taste Test." *The Village Voice*, May 5, 1980, p. 83.

Ammann, Jean-Christophe, ed. *Sandro Chia, Francesco Clemente, Enzo Cucchi, Nicola de Maria, Luigi Ontani, Mimmi Paladino, Ernesto Tatafiore*. Kunsthalle Basel, Basel, 1980.

"Italienische Kunst heute." *Kunstforum*, March 1980, passim.

Oliva, Achille Bonito. "An Interview with Achille Bonito Oliva." *Flash Art*, Summer 1980, pp. 8–9.

Pincus-Witten, Robert. "Entries: If Even in Fractions." *Arts Magazine*, September 1980, pp. 116–119.

Larson, Kay. "Bad Boys at Large! The Three C's Take on New York." *The Village Voice*, September 17–23, 1980, p. 35.

Zimmer, William. "Italians Iced." *The SoHo Weekly News*, October 8–14, 1980, p. 45.

Lawson, Thomas. Review. *Flash Art*, November 1980, p. 43.

Francesco Clemente. Padiglione d'Arte Contemporanea di Milano, Milan, 1980.

Ammann, Jean-Christophe; Groot, Paul; Heynen, Pieter; and Zumbrink, Jan. "Un altre art?" *Museumjournaal*, December 1980, cover, pp. 292–293.

Oliva, Achille Bonito. *La Transavangarde Italienne*. Giancarlo Politi, Milan, 1980.

Chi pinge figura, si non puo' essere lei non la puo' porre. Adyar, India, 1980.

Lambarelli, R. Review. *Flash Art/Heute Kunst*, June/July 1980, p. 60.

———. Review. *Art & Artists*, February 1980, p. 38.

Nadelman, Cynthia. Review. *Artnews*, December 1980, p. 193.

Rickey, Carrie. Review. *Artforum*, December 1980, pp. 70–71.

Curtis, C. "Straddling Grace and Decadence." *Artweek*, September 12, 1981, p. 16.

"Bericht aus London." *Kunstwerk*, Vol. 34, No. 6, 1981, p. 54.

Franzke, A. "7 junge Künstler aus Italien." *Pantheon*, January/March 1981, p. 8.

Oliva, Achille Bonito. "Francesco Clemente." *Domus*, January 1981, pp. 52–53.

deAk, Edit. "A Chameleon in a State of Grace." *Artforum*, February 1981, pp. 36–41.

Casademont, Joan. Review. *Artforum*, April 1981, p. 65.

Zaya. "Conversación con Francesco Clemente: sustancia de lo imaginario." *Guadalimar*, No. 56, Madrid, Spain, pp. 14–15.

"Clemente in SoHo." *Connaissance des Arts*, May 1981, p. 35.

Larson, Kay. "Obsessed—and Repelled—by the Past." *Artnews*, May 1981, p. 76.

Levin, Kim. "The Miniature Marauder." *The Village Voice*, May 20–26, 1981, p. 90.

Larson, Kay. "Between a Rock and a Soft Place." *New York Magazine*, June 1, 1981, pp. 56–58.

Ricard, Rene. "Not About Julian Schnabel." *Artforum*, June 1981, pp. 74–80.

Kramer, Hilton. "Art: Expressionism from Italy Arrives." *The New York Times*, June 5, 1981, p. C19.

Payant, René. "From Landuage to Landuage." *Parachute* (Montréal), Summer 1981, pp. 27–33.

"Newsbreakers." *Cover*, Spring/Summer 1981, p. 16.

Kramer, Hilton. "Expressionism Returns to Painting." *The New York Times*, July 12, 1981, Sec. 2, p. 1.

Armstrong, Richard. Review. *Artforum*, September 1981, pp. 83–86.

Lolis, Merope. Review. *Arts Magazine*, September 1981, p. 23.

Perrone, Jeff. "Boy Do I Love Art or What?" *Arts Magazine*, September 1981, pp. 72–78.

Rouzade, Jean, and Laugier, Emile. "Francesco Clemente change de style chaque matin comme on enfile un costume." *Actuel*, September 1981, pp. 82–83.

Ratcliff, Carter. "The End of the American Era." *Saturday Review*, September 1981, pp. 42–43.

"Malerei '81: Triumph der Wilden." *art* (Hamburg), October 1981, pp. 22–43.

Trucco, Terry. "Sensations of the Year." *Portfolio*, September/October 1981, pp. 42–47.

Blau, Douglas. "Francesco Clemente." *Flash Art*, October/November 1981, p. 54.

Phillips, Deborah C. Review. *images & issues*, Fall 1981, pp. 57–58.

Wilson, William. "Clemente: The Uses of Naivete." *Los Angeles Times*, November 2, 1981, Part VI, p. 1.

Nadelman, Cynthia. Review. *Artnews*, September 1981, p. 160.

Figures: Forms and Expressions. The Buffalo Fine Arts Academy, Buffalo, New York, 1981.

Hunter, Sam. *Aspects of Post-Modernism.* The Squibb Gallery, Princeton, 1981.

Francesco Clemente, Pinxit. Anthony d'Offay, London, 1981.

Vadel, Bernard Lamarche, and Enrici, Michel. Translated by Pierre-François Marietti. "Entretien avec Achille Bonito Oliva." *Artistes*, October/November 1981, pp. 17–25.

White, Robin. "Interview by Robin White at Crown Point Press." Oakland, California, 1981.

Brown, Kathan. Essay in *Italians and Other Americans.* Crown Point Press, Oakland, California, 1981.

Glueck, Grace. "Fresh Talent, New Buyers Brighten Art Outlook in U.S." *International Herald Tribune*, November 19, 1981, p. 5.

Curtis, Cathy. "Clemente Paintings Stay in the Mind." *North East Bay Independent and Gazette* (Berkeley edition), August 13, 1981.

———. "Straddling Grace and Decadence." *Artweek*, September 12, 1981.

Marchel-Workman, Andree. "Italian Art in the Bay Area." *West Art*, October 9, 1981.

Lewallen, Constance. "MATRIX: Clemente, Eno, Hagemeyer." University Art Museum, Berkeley, July/August 1981, p. 2.

Zimmer, William. Review. *The Soho News*, October 6, 1981.

Castle, Ted. "A Bouquet of Mistakes." *Flash Art*, Summer 1982, pp. 54–55.

Gast, Dwight V. "Contemporary Art in Florence: Not Just a Wet Canvas." *Daily American*, January 3–4, 1982, p. 9.

"On Tape: Henry Geldzahler, Commissioner of New York City's Department of Cultural Affairs." *Express,* Spring 1982, pp. 4–5.

deAk, Edit, and Cortez, Diego. "Baby Talk." *Flash Art,* May 1982, pp. 34–38.

Cone, Michele. "A Saint's Foot, a Moral House, and Two Voyeurs." *ArtExpress,* January/February 1982, pp. 34–35.

Smith, Roberta. "Drawing Fire." *The Village Voice,* August 17, 1982, p. 74.

Russell, John. "Art: Drawings, Reticent and Bold, at the Modern." *The New York Times,* July 30, 1982, p. C24.

Larson, Kay. "The Powers of Paper." *New York Magazine,* August 23, 1982, p. 74.

Bourdon, David. "Battling the Masters." *Geo,* August 1982, pp. 30–45.

Panicelli, Ida. Translated by Meg Shore. "Italian Art Now: An American Perspective, Guggenheim Museum." *Artforum,* June 1982, p. 83.

Kontova, Helena. "From Performance to Painting." *Flash Art,* February/March 1982, pp. 16–21.

von Graevenitz, Antje. Essay in *kunst nu/kunst unserer zeit.* Groninger Museum, Groningen, 1982, p. 5.

Ratcliff, Carter. "On Iconography and Some Italians." *Art in America,* September 1982, pp. 152–159.

Russell, John. "A Palace of Pleasure." *The New York Times,* July 11, 1982, Sec. 2, p. 1.

Fuchs, R. H. Foreword to *Documenta 7.* Paul Dierichs GmbH & Co., Kassel, 1982.

Frackman, Noel, and Kaufmann, Ruth. "Documenta 7: The Dialogue and a Few Asides." *Arts Magazine,* October 1982, pp. 91–97.

Marzorati, Gerald. "Documenta 7." *Portfolio,* September/October 1982, pp. 92–95.

Cummings, Paul. "Interview: Norman Dubrow Talks with Paul Cummings." *Drawing,* January/February 1982, pp. 107–111.

Di Felice, Attanasio. "The Italian Moderns." *Attenzione,* March 1982, pp. 62–63.

———. "Painting with a Past: New Art from Italy." *Portfolio,* March/April 1982, pp. 94–99.

Berger, Danny. "Francesco Clemente at the Metropolitan: An Interview." *The Print Collector's Newsletter,* March/April 1982, pp. 11–13.

Moore, John M. "The Return of the Emotive." *Connaissance des Arts,* March 1982, pp. 54–61.

deAk, Edit. "Francesco Clemente." *Interview,* April 1982, pp. 68–70.

Raynor, Vivien. "A Taste of the New and the Old at Atheneum." *The New York Times,* March 21, 1982, Sec. 23, p. 22.

Hoelterhoff, Manuela. "Two Homages to the Long-Lost Italian Muse." *The Wall Street Journal,* April 23, 1982, p. 27.

Schjeldahl, Peter. "Treachery on the High C's." *The Village Voice*, April 27, 1982, p. 96.

Strasser, Catherine. "Francesco Clemente le son du corps." *artpress*, May 1982, pp. 24–25.

Sosnoff, Martin. Introduction to *Homo Sapiens: the many images.* The Aldrich Museum of Contemporary Art, Ridgefield, Connecticut, 1982.

Tucker, Marcia. "An Iconography of Recent Figurative Painting: Sex, Death, Violence, and the Apocalypse." *Artforum*, June 1982, pp. 70–75.

Stevens, Mark. "Revival of Realism: Art's Wild Young Turks." *Newsweek*, June 7, 1982, pp. 64–70.

Russell, John. "Art: Marlborough Offers Sampler of 17 Painters." *The New York Times*, June 11, 1982, p. C26.

Cortez, Diego. *The Pressure to Paint.* Marlborough Gallery, Inc., New York, 1982.

Tomkins, Calvin. "The Art World: Seminar." *The New Yorker*, June 7, 1982, pp. 120–125.

Smith, Roberta. "Art: Group Flex." *The Village Voice*, June 22, 1982, p. 106.

Larson, Kay. "Art: Pressure Points." *New York Magazine*, June 28, 1982, pp. 58–59.

Grosskopf, Annegret. "Documenta 7." *Stern*, June 16–23, 1982, pp. 40–57.

Phillips, Deborah C. "No Island Is an Island: New York Discovers the Europeans." *Artnews*, October 1982, pp. 66–71.

Joachimides, Christos, and Rosenthal, Norman. Foreword to *Zeitgeist.* Berlin, 1982.

Kruger, Barbara. Review of "New Work on Paper 2" at The Museum of Modern Art, New York. *Artforum*, November 1982, pp. 76–77.

Liebmann, Lisa. "Paris—Francesco Clemente, Daniel Templon." *Artforum*, November 1982, p. 83.

Taylor, Paul. " 'Vision in Disbelief,' Fourth Biennale of Sydney." *Artforum*, October 1982, p. 79.

Silverthorne, Jeanne. " 'The Pressure to Paint,' Marlborough Gallery." *Artforum*, October 1982, pp. 67–68.

Clarke, John R. "Up Against the Wall, Transavanguardia!" *Arts Magazine*, December 1982, pp. 76–81.

Grosskopf, Annegret. "Bomben-Stimmung '82." *Stern*, October 14–20, 1982, pp. 186–203.

Harrison, Helen A. "Showing How and What to Draw." *The New York Times*, December 5, 1982, Sec. 21, p. 36.

Crone, Rainer. Essay in *Francesco Clemente: "Il viaggiatore napoletano."* Paul Maenz, Cologne, 1982.

Russell, John. "A Big Berlin Show That Misses the Mark." *The New York Times*, December 5, 1982, Sec. 2, p. 33.

Son, 1984.
Oil/linen; 112″ x 91″.
Albright-Knox Art Gallery, Buffalo,
New York. George B. and Jenny R.
Mathews Fund, 1985.
Photo: Biff Henrich.

BOMB, November 1982, New York. (Illus.: *Spes*, p. 48.)

Crone, Rainer. *Francesco Clemente Watercolors*. Bruno Bischofberger, Zürich, 1982.

Rose, Bernice. *New Work on Paper* (exhibition catalogue includes reproductions of works by Jonathan Borofsky, Francesco Clemente, Mario Merz, A. R. Penck and Giuseppe Penone). The Museum of Modern Art, New York, 1982.

Argan, Guilio Carlo, and Oliva, Achille Bonito. "Avanguardia e trans-avanguardia" (dialogue). *Iterarte 24*, June 1982, pp. 3–32.

Politi, Giancarlo. "Documenta." *Flash Art*, November 1982, pp. 34–37.

Ammann, Jean-Christophe. "Documenta: Reality & Desire." *Flash Art*, November 1982, pp. 37–39.

Politi, Giancarlo. "Venice Biennale." *Flash Art*, November 1982, pp. 46–48.

Cocuccioni, Enrico. "Avantgarde-Transavantgarde." *Flash Art*, November 1982, pp. 70–71.

Robbins, D. A. "The 'Meaning' of 'New'—the '70s/'80s Axis: An Interview with Diego Cortez." *Arts Magazine*, January 1983, pp. 116–121.

Januszczak, Waldemar. "Arte Italiana 1960–1982." *Flash Art*, January 1983, pp. 67–68.

Francis, Mark, ed. *Francesco Clemente: The Fourteen Stations*. The Whitechapel Art Gallery, London, 1983. Published in France, Galerie d'Art Contemporain des Musées de Nice, Nice, 1983. Exhibition catalogue did not include *Fortune* and *Perseverance*.

"Resident Artists 1982." *Skowhegan School of Painting and Sculpture: Summer 1983*. Skowhegan, Maine, 1983.

Taylor, John Russell. "Tearing Passion to Tatters." *The Times* (London), January 11, 1983.

Cork, Richard. "Art on View: New York in Siege and Snow." *The Standard* (London), January 27, 1983, p. 21.

Bastian, Heiner. *Chia, Clemente, Cucchi—Bilder* (catalogue for exhibition at Kunsthalle Bielefeld). Berlin, 1982, essay by Wolfgang Max Faust.

Clare, Henry. Review. *The Glasgow Herald*, January 13, 1983.

Burr, James. "Making a Little Go a Long Way." *Apollo*, January 1983, p. 62.

Anderson, Alexandra. "Art Boom in New York: The Sudden Arrival of Francesco Clemente." *Harpers & Queen* (London), February 1983, pp. 134–135.

Fawcett, Anthony, and Withers, Jane. "Francesco Clemente, Artist as Sage." *The Face*, February 1983.

Feaver, William. "Quick and Slow." *The Observer* (London), January 30, 1983.

Clarke, Michael. "Free Forms." *The Times Educational Supplement* (London), January 28, 1983.

Gooding, Mel. "Francesco Clemente." *Arts Review* (London), January 21, 1983.

Bastian, Heiner. "Samtale med Francesco Clemente" (interview). *Louisiana Revy* (Humlebaek, Denmark), June 1983, pp. 40–44, 52–54, 56.

Shone, Richard. "New York—Some Recent Exhibitions." *The Burlington Magazine*, July 1983, pp. 450–451.

Silver, Ken. "Figures from Italy." *Gentlemen's Quarterly*, October 1983, pp. 246–249.

Blackall, Judith. "Francesco Clemente—Two Exhibitions in London." *Art Network*, Autumn 1983, pp. 67–68.

Exner, Julian. "Wildheit and Witz; Doppel Austellungen: Barry Flannagan und Francesco Clemente." *Frankfurter Rundschau*, February 2, 1983.

Compton, Michael. *New Art*. The Tate Gallery, London, 1983.

Brown, Julia, and Johnson, Bridget, eds. *The First Show, Painting and Sculpture from Eight Collections*, with essays and interviews by Julian Brown, Pontus Hulten, and Susan C. Larsen. Museum of Contemporary Art, Los Angeles, 1983.

Francesco Clemente Paintings. Akira Ikeda Gallery, Nagoya and Tokyo, 1983.

Kuspit, Donald. Review. *Art in America*, November 1983, p. 227.

M. P. "Tutto E Cosi Sia." *L'Uomo Vogure* (Milan), October 1983, pp. 342–343.

Ars 83 Helsinki, including essays by Matti Ranki, Pauli Paaermaa, Leena Peltola, Yrjana Levanto, Mats B. J. O. Mallander, and Barbara J. London. Ateneumin Taidemuseo, Helsinki, 1983.

Expressive Malerie nach Picasso. Galerie Beyeler, Basel, 1983.

Det Italienska Transavantgardet, with an introduction by Cecilia Stam. The Boibrono Gallery, Stockholm, 1983.

Stevens, Mark. "A Renaissance for European Artists." *Newsweek International*, January 2, 1984, pp. 56–57.

"Italia Contemporanea." *Harper's Bazaar en Español*, February 1984, pp. 94–97.

Temin, Christine. "The ICA's Barely Installations." *The Boston Globe*, January 26, 1984, p. 47.

Goldberg, RoseLee. "Two Sides of the Brain: Molissa Fenley's *Hemispheres*," *Artforum*, January 1984, pp. 57–60.

Sussman, Elisabeth. *Currents, Francesco Clemente*. Institute of Contemporary Art, Boston, 1984.

Tully, Judd. "A New Expression." *Horizon*, January/February 1984, pp. 38–47.

Madoff, Steven Henry. Review. "Ars 83 Helsinki." *Artnews*, January 1984, pp. 120–123.

Crone, Rainer; Felix, Zdenek; and Grisebach, Lucius. *Francesco Clemente, Pastelle 1974–1983*. Munich, 1984.

Modern Expressionists. Sidney Janis Gallery, New York, 1984.

Kaplan, Steven. *Totem.* Bonnier Gallery, Charles Cowles Gallery, Germans Van Eck, New York, 1984.

Templon, Daniel. *Daniel Templon 1978–1983.* Paris, 1984.

B., Mats. *Det Italienska Transavantgardet.* Stockholm Art Fair and Lunds Konsthall, Stockholm and Lund, Sweden, 1984.

Painting Now. Akira Ikeda Gallery, Nagoya, 1984.

Sundgren, Nils Petter. "Den Nya Italienska Konsten." *Manads Journalen* (Stockholm), March 1984, pp. 45–53.

Rogozinski, Luciana. "La Position Crépusculaire, notes sur l'art italien aujourd'hui." *Parachute* (Montréal), March/April/May 1984, pp. 4–18.

Politi, Giancarlo. "Francesco Clemente." *Flash Art,* April/May 1984, cover, pp. 12–21.

Ginsberg, Allen, and Clemente, Francesco. *The White Shroud.* Kunsthalle Basel, Basel, 1984.

Francesco Clemente. Ascan Crone Gallery, Hamburg, 1984.

Via New York, with essays by Robert Pincus-Witten and Phillip Evans-Clark. Musée d'Art Contemporain, Montréal, 1984.

Contemporary Italian Masters, with essays by Henry Geldzahler and Judith Russi Kirshner. Chicago Council on Fine Arts and The Renaissance Society of the University of Chicago. Chicago, 1984.

McShine, Kynaston. *An International Survey of Recent Painting and Sculpture.* The Museum of Modern Art, New York, 1984.

Wilson, William. Review. *Los Angeles Times,* June 8, 1984.

Norklun, Kathi. "Francesco Clemente at James Corcoran Gallery." *L.A. Weekly,* June 22, 1984.

The Human Condition, The SFMMA Biennial III. San Francisco Museum of Modern Art, San Francisco, 1984.

Freeman, Phyllis; Himmel, Eric; Pavese, Edith; and Yarowsky, Anne. *New Art.* New York, 1984.

Diacono, Mario. *Verso una nuova iconographia.* Reggio Emilia, 1984.

Bourdon, David. "The Go-Betweens." *Vogue,* September 1984, p. 98.

Painting Now, with an essay by Nobuyuki Hiromoto. Kitakyushu Municipal Museum of Art, Kitakyushu, Japan, 1984.

Content: A Contemporary Focus, 1974–1984, with essays by Miranda McClintic, Howard Fox and Phyllis Rosenzweig. The Hirshhorn Museum and Sculpture Garden, Washington, D.C., 1984.

Rosc '84. The Guinness Hop Store, Dublin, 1984.

Idone, Carol. Review. *Flash Art,* November 1984, p. 46.

Keziere, Russell. "Tiresias Unbound." *Vanguard,* September 1984, pp. 8–12.

Francesco Clemente in Belfast. Arts Council of Northern Ireland, Belfast, 1984.

Oliva, Achille Bonito. *Dialoghi d'artista.* Milan, 1984.

Haenlein, Carl. *Francesco Clemente.* Kestner Gesellschaft, Hannover, 1984.

Curiger, Bice. *Looks et Tenebrae.* Peter Blum Edition, New York and Zürich, 1984.

Szeeman, Harald. "Im Jardin d'amour." *Lo Spazio Umano,* October/December 1984, pp. 7–17.

Heartney, Eleanor. "Images and Impressions." *Arts,* December 1984, pp. 118–121.

Collaborations. Akira Ikeda Gallery, Tokyo, 1985.

Martin, Henry. "Inside Europe: Italy." *Artnews,* February 1985, pp. 60–62.

Shone, Richard. Review. *The Burlington Magazine,* February 1985, p. 115.

Thomson, Richard. Review. *The Burlington Magazine,* February 1985, pp. 114–115.

Gardner, Paul. "Gargoyles, Goddesses and Faces in the Crowd." *Artnews,* March 1985, pp. 52–59.

Brenson, Michael. "Human Figure Is Back in Unlikely Guises." *The New York Times,* January 13, 1985, Sec. 2, p. 1.

Sischy, Ingrid. "East Sets West Sets East." *Artforum,* January 1985, pp. 59–75.

Kontova, Helena, and Politi, Giancarlo. "Paris Biennale and Turin's New Museum." *Flash Art,* April/May 1985, pp. 36–37.

Kent, Sarah. "Critical Images." *Flash Art,* April/May 1985, pp. 23–27.

Goldberger, Paul. "The Palladium." *The New York Times,* May 20, 1985, p. B3.

McGuigan, Cathleen, and Malone, Maggie. "Bitten by the Collecting Bug." *Newsweek,* May 13, 1985, pp. 90–94.

McGuigan, Cathleen. "A Garden of Disco Delights." *Newsweek,* May 20, 1985, p. 76.

Rezvin, Phillip. *The Wall Street Journal,* April 8, 1985, p. 14.

———. *The Wall Street Journal,* April 11, 1985, p. 28.

Hawthorne, Don. "Saatchi and Saatchi Go Public." *Artnews,* May 1985, pp. 72–81.

Russell, John. *The New York Times,* April 5, 1985, p. C19.

Hughes, Robert. "Symbolist with Roller Skates." *Time,* April 22, 1985, p. 68.

Bourdon, David. "Eye to I." *Vogue,* April 1985, p. 90.

Pohlen, Annelie. "Cosmic Visions from North and South." *Artforum,* March 1985, pp. 76–81.

Guenther, Bruce. *States of War.* Seattle Art Museum, Seattle, 1985.

DIALOG. Gulbenkian Foundation, Lisbon, 1985.

Bastian, Heiner. *7000 Eichen.* Berlin, 1985.

Selections from the William J. Hokin Collection. Museum of Contemporary Art, Chicago, 1985.

Francesco Clemente Prints 1981–1985. The Metropolitan Museum of Art, New York, 1985.

Day, Holliday T. *New Art of Italy.* Joslyn Art Museum, Omaha, and The Contemporary Arts Center, Cincinnati, 1985.

Koepplin, Dieter. "Suchen sie nicht nach der Bedeutung." *Nordschweiz/Basler Volksblatt,* July 13, 1985.

Pincus-Witten, Robert. "Entries: Becoming American." *Arts,* October 1985, pp. 101–103.

Kuspit, Donald. "Cumulus from America." *Parkett,* 1985, pp. 93–99.

Cone, Michele. *Flash Art,* Summer 1985, p. 55.

Daly, Michael. "The Comeback Kids." *New York Magazine,* July 22, 1985, pp. 28–29.

Ormond, Mark, and Adams, Marianna. *Francesco Clemente.* The John and Mable Ringling Museum of Art, Sarasota, 1985.

Russell, John. "Modern Art Museums, the Surprise Is Gone." *The New York Times,* August 4, 1985, Sec. 2, p. 1.

Ratcliff, Carter. *Art in America,* October 1985, pp. 9–13.

McEvilley, Thomas. Review. *Artforum,* October 1985, p. 123.

Auping, Michael. *Francesco Clemente.* New York, 1985.

Gorgoni, Gianfranco. *Beyond the Canvas.* New York, 1985.

Isozaki, Arato. "The Palladium." *Domus,* November 1985, pp. 36–41.

Paparoni, Demetrio. "Collaborations Basquiat, Clemente, Warhol." *Tema Celeste,* November 1985, pp. 20–23.

Stevens, Mark. *Newsweek,* December 16, 1985, pp. 76–80.

Gimelson, Deborah. "Francesco Clemente." *Art and Auction,* 1985, p. 36.

Wolff, Theodore F. *The Christian Science Monitor,* October 10, 1985, p. 34.

Oliva, Achille Bonito. *La Critica d'arte come arte della critica.* Nuova Prearo Editore, 1985.

Wolff, Theodore F. *The Christian Science Monitor,* June 24, 1985, p. 23.

Clarke, John R. "Circuses and Bread." *Arts,* October 1985, pp. 34–39.

Carnegie International, with essays by Rudi Fuchs, Germano Celant, Jannis Kounellis, Per Kirkeby, Johannes Gachnang, Bazon Brock, Nicholas Serota, Benjamin H. D. Buchloh, Hal Foster, Donald Kuspit, Mark Rosenthal, Peter Schjeldahl and Thomas McEvilley. Museum of Art, Carnegie Institute, Pittsburgh, 1985.

Temin, Christine. *The Boston Globe,* September 27, 1985, p. 64.

Tomkins, Calvin. *The New Yorker,* July 22, 1985, pp. 64–66.

La Nouvelle Biennale de Paris, with essays by Georges Boudaille, Jean-Pierre Fay, Alanna Heiss, Gerald Gassio-Talabot, Achille Bonito Oliva, Pierre Courcelles and Marie Luise Syring. Paris, 1985.

Fuchs, Rudi. *Ouverture.* Castello di Rivoli, Turin, 1985.

Morgan, Stuart. *Artscribe,* December/January 1985/6, p. 72.

Clemente, Francesco. BOMB, Winter 1986, pp. 30–31.

Hawthorne, Don. "Prints from the Alchemist's Laboratory." *Artnews,* February 1985, pp. 89–95.

Brenson, Michael. *The New York Times,* January 5, 1986, Sec. 2, p. 1.

Groot, Paul. "Alchemy and the Rediscovery of the Human Figure in Recent Art." *Flash Art,* February/March 1986, pp. 42–43.

Nadelman, Cynthia. Review. *Artnews,* March 1986, pp. 115–116.

Stavitsky, Gail. "The 1985 Carnegie International." *Arts,* March 1986, pp. 58–59.

Cooke, Lynne. *In Tandem.* The Whitechapel Art Gallery, London, 1986.

Murphy, Bernice. *Francesco Clemente Pastels.* Adelaide Festival of Arts, Adelaide, 1986.

Findsen, Owen. "Italians Redefine Modern Art." *The Cincinnati Enquirer,* April 3, 1986, Sec. D, p. 1.

Stein, Jerry. "New Italian Show Offering a Blitz of Color at CAC." *The Cincinnati Post,* April 4, 1986, p. 6B.

Caldwell, John. "Creating Taste." *Dialogue,* March/April 1986, pp. 14–16.

Kass, Ray. "Current Milestones." *Dialogue,* March/April 1986, pp. 17–19.

Taylor, Paul. *Flash Art,* February/March 1986, p. 52.

van der Marck, Jan. "Report from Pittsburgh." *Art in America,* May 1986, pp. 49–55.

Clemente, Francesco. *Zibaldone,* No. 1, 1986, cover.

Tuchman, Phyllis. *New York Newsday,* April 20, 1986, Part II, p. 11.

Skrapits, Joseph C. "Strokes of Genius." *Attenzione,* June 1986, pp. 23–29.

Francesco Clemente Women & Men. Akira Ikeda Gallery, Tokyo, 1986.

Clemente, Francesco; Shapiro, David; Crone, Rainer; and Pellizzi, Francesco. *Parkett,* 1986, cover, pp. 16–81.

Staeck, Klaus; Schneckenburger, Manfred; Werner, Klaus; and Brock, Bazon, eds. *Ohne die rose tun wir's nicht für Joseph Beuys.* Heidelberg, 1986.

Malerie, 1986, pp. 62–72.

Crone, Rainer. *Flash Art,* Summer 1986, p. 30.

Kontova, Helena, and Politi, Giancarlo. "Interview." *Flash Art,* Summer 1986, cover, pp. 31–38.

Clemente, Francesco. *The Pondicherry Pastels.* London and Madras, 1986.

Felshin, Nina, and McEvilley, Thomas. *Focus on the Image.* New York, 1986.

Oliva, Achille Bonito. "Figurabila." *Tema Celeste,* May 1986, pp. 33–42.

Rosenthal, Mark. *Philadelphia Collects Art Since 1940.* Philadelphia, 1986.

Pakesch, Peter, ed. *Die Wahlverwandtschaften Zitate.* Graz, 1986.

UNTITLED, 1984. Oil/canvas; 108″ x 188″. Collection of Thomas Ammann, Zürich. Courtesy Sperone Westwater, New York. Photo: Dorothy Zeidman.